OCCUPYING THE SUMMIT

The Guide to Successful Retirement Planning

Robert W. Shaffer

Wordware Publishing, Inc.

Library of Congress Cataloging-in-Publication Data

Shaffer, Robert, W.
   Occupying the summit : the guide to successful retirement planning / Robert W. Shaffer.

   Includes index.
   ISBN 1-55622-102-9
   1. Retirement—United States—Planning. 2. Retirees—United States—Finance, Personal. 3. Retirement income—United States—Planning.   I. Title.
   HQ1062.S527   1989   646.7'9—do19   89-5322

© 1989 Wordware Publishing, Inc.

All Rights Reserved

1506 Capital Ave.
Plano, Texas 75074

No part of this book may be reproduced in any form or by any means without permission in writing from Wordware Publishing, Inc.

Printed in the United States of America

ISBN 1-55622-102-9

10 9 8 7 6 5 4 3 2 1
8901

All inquiries for volume purchases of this book should be addressed to Wordware Publishing, Inc., at the above address. Telephone inquiries may be made by calling:

(214) 423-0090

Contents

	Page
Introduction	1

Section I
Financial Independence

Chapter 1 — Facts	7
Determining Your Financial Status	9
Net Worth Statement	9
What Other Assets are You Likely to Acquire?	10
What Type of Retirement Do You Want?	11
Skill Inventory	11
Mission	11
Recreation Desired	11
Intellectual and Social Needs	12
Where Do You Want to Live?	12
Should You Remain in Your Present Home?	12
How Do You Select a Retirement Location?	13
What Type of Housing Do You Want?	14
Committing Your Ideas to Paper	16
Chapter 2 — Assumptions	17
Inflation	19
Earnings on Investments	20
Where are You in Your Career Progression?	20
How Long Do You Want to Work?	21
Longevity Outlook	21
Increase in Social Security Benefits	22
Chapter 3 — Your Plan — Preretirees	23
Pension Income	26
Social Security Benefits	26
Retirement Living Costs	28
Housing	29
Food	29
Clothing	29
Transportation	29
Recreation	29
Life Insurance	30
Medical Expenses	30

Contributions to Charity 30
Gifts 30
Miscellaneous and Contingency 30
   Inflation-Free Expenses 31
   Inflation-Impacted Expenses 31
Income Tax on Pension and Social Security Benefits 31
Savings Required for Retirement 31
After-Tax Earnings on Investments 32
   Marginal Tax Rate 32
Investments Required 33
Analysis of Financial Plan for Retirement 33
   Inflation 34
   The Savings Program 35
   Living With the Assumptions 36

Chapter 4 — Your Plan — Retirees 45
Typical Retirement Situations 47
   Limited Income — Limited Consumption 47
   Sufficient Income — Phobic Underconsumption 47
   Sufficient Income — Erratic Consumption 48
   Excellent Income — Conspicuous Consumption 48
Preparing Your Basic Plan 48
   Dick and Jane 49
      Dick and Jane's Budget 50
      Review of Their Budget 55
      Learning from Their Plan 55
Preparing Your Financial Plan 57

Chapter 5 — Investment Alternatives and Strategies 59
Part 1: Introduction 61
   The Fable of Bill the Baker 61
   Analysis 63
Investment Terminology 65
   Loans 65
   Purchasing an Interest in a Business 65
   Purchasing Tangible Assets 65
   Marginal Tax Rate 66
   Leverage 66
      Example 1 67
      Example 2 67
Part 2: Investment Alternatives 67
   Loans 68
   Purchasing an Interest in a Business 71
      Common Stock 71

Preferred Stock	71
Limited Partnership	72
Purchase of Tangible Assets	73
Conclusions	73
Part 3: Investment Strategy	73
Attributes of the Skilled Investor	73
Knowledge	74
Imagination	74
Decisiveness	75
The Discipline to Save	75
Impact of Age	76
Assumed Inflation Rate	76
Marginal Tax Rate	76
Tax Code Provisions	77
Leverage	77
Diversification	77
Investments Strategy Outline	77
"Coin Flip" Investment Scenario	78
Risk-Reward Grid	82
Liquidity	83
Emergencies	83
Investment Flexibility	83
Dollar Risk	83
Purchasing Power Reward	84
George's Investments	85
Bonds	86
Stocks	86
XYZ Company	86
Real Estate — Residential	87
Gold	89
Part 4: Advisory Services	90
Mutual Funds	90
Stock and Bond Brokers	92
Market Letters and Financial Publications	92
Investment Counselors	93
Tax Attorneys, Accountants, Bankers	93
Trusts	93
Criteria for Picking Advisors	94
Summary	94
Chapter 6 — Contingency and Alternative Plans	**97**
Contingency Plans	99
Inflation	99
Longevity	99

Promotion	100
Health	100
Income Taxes and Investments	100
Inheritance	100
Death	100
Alternate Plans	101
Retirement Age	101
Retirement Life Style	101
Retirement Housing	101
Dealing With an Investment Deficit	102
Estate Planning	102

Chapter 7 — Monitoring Progress 105
    Annual Inventory 107
    Annual Update 108
    Keeping the Proper Perspective 109

Section II
Life With a Purpose

Chapter 1 — The Rites of Passage 113
    Historical Rites of Passage 115
    The Lengthening Life Span and Financial Independence 116
    The Retirement Party's Implied Message 116
    Planning for Change 118

Chapter 2 — On Becoming a Retiree 119
    The Hierarachy of Needs 121
        Physiological Needs 122
        Safety and Security 122
        Social or Affiliation Needs 123
        Esteem 123
        Self-Actualization 124
    Motivation Factors 124
        Status 125
        Recognition and Self-Actualization 125
    Meeting Our Needs in Retirement 125

Chapter 3 — Reach Out and Touch Someone 129
    The Need for Social Interaction 131
    Enhancing Social Skills 131
        Developing Multiple Interests 132
        Turning Acquaintances into Friends 132
            Improving Communication Skills 132

Effective Listening	132
Body Language	133
Semantics	133
Comprehension	133
Showing Interest in the Other Person	13
Sources for Friendship	134
Original Circle of Friends	134
New Acquaintances	134
Family	134

Chapter 4 — The Gap is the Problem ... 137
Recognizing the Gap ... 139
    Pete's Story ... 140
Closing the Gap ... 141
    Pete's New Value System ... 142

Chapter 5 — Who am I? ... 143
Typical Roles ... 145
    Explorer ... 145
    Provider ... 146
    Competitor ... 146
    Advisor ... 147
    Reaper ... 148
Discovering the Real You ... 149
    Recalling Your Past ... 149
    Listing Your Skills and Strengths ... 149
        Bill's Story ... 150
        Bill Takes Inventory ... 152

Chapter 6 — Why am I? ... 157
Intellectual Stimulation ... 159
    Systematic Pursuit of Knowledge ... 159
    Advisory and/or Teaching Activities ... 160
    Hobbies and Crafts ... 160
    Intellectual Games ... 161
    Political Activity ... 161
    Traveling ... 161
    Investments ... 162
    A Second or Continued Career ... 162
Spiritual Stimulation ... 162
Physical Needs ... 163
Recreation ... 164
    Revisiting Bill ... 164
        Golf ... 166

Bridge	166
Travel	166
Dancing	166
Investments	166
Art	166
Reading	167
Horticulture	167

Chapter 7 — How? 171
   Strategic Planning 173
   Tactical Planning 174
   Operational Planning 175

Section III
Wellness

Chapter 1 — What is Wellness? 179
   Achieving a Balance 181
   Degree of Wellness 182
   Taking Time to Smell the Roses 183

Chapter 2 — Physical Health 185
   Increased Life Expectancy 187
   Cardiovascular Functions 188
   Cardiovascular Degeneration 188
      Placque in the Arteries 190
      Hypertension 191
      Lack of Exercise 192
      Smoking 192
      Stress 192
   Preparing for a Quality Life 193

Chapter 3 — Emotional Health 195
   Reactions to Stress 197
      Emotional Pain 197
      The Fight or Flight Syndrome 198
      Illness 199
   Stressful Life Events 199
   Retirement as a Source of Stress 202
   Postretirement Stress 202
      Boredom 203
      Isolation 203
      Role Ambiguity 203

    The Stress Management Program 204
        Identifying Stressful Events 205
        Predicting Future Stressful Events 205
        Avoiding Pain 206
        Scheduling Pain 206
        Increasing Adaptive Capacity 206
            Physical Vigor 207
            Mental Strength 207
            Spiritual Vitality 208

Chapter 4 — Spiritual Health 211
    The Universality of Belief 213
    Understanding Our Being 213
    The Programming of Our Intellect 214
    Reprogramming Our Intellect 215
    Formulating Our Ultimate Concern 217
    Working Toward Wellness 217

Chapter 5 — Your Plan for Wellness 219
    Determining Your Present Condition 221
    Planning for Improvement 221
        Establishing Goals 222
        Updating Annually 222

Conclusions 223
Bibliography for Recommended Reading 225
Appendix — Work Sheets 231
Index 269

Introduction

The purpose of this book is to illustrate how to plan your retirement. Those who read it and apply the principles, will have a better chance of enjoying their harvest years. Robert Browning wrote: "The best is yet to be; the last of life, for which the first was made." A bountiful harvest requires toil; one must plant, cultivate, and nurture before reaping. Retirement, like agriculture, requires preparation and work before the harvest.

Discussions with numerous retired people and an extensive review of material on the subject led me to the conclusion that to enjoy retirement to the fullest, one should possess (1) financial independence, (2) activities that will give a sense that life has a purpose, and (3) good health. I have encountered many retired people who say, and give every indication, that they are happy even though they lack one or more of the above ingredients. Yet in all cases they admit that their satisfaction would be greater if they had the missing element.

Our preretirement thinking generally falls into one or more of the following categories:

1. *Escape from drudgery* Some find their present job unpleasant. They picture retirement years filled with traveling, fishing, golfing, and other forms of recreation. To them the grass is greener on the other side of the fence, and they think about retiring FROM something rather than TO something. These individuals will probably be as unhappy in retirement as they are in their present job because they fail to anticipate the changes needed for an enjoyable retirement.
2. *Gloomy deprivation* Others simply refuse to face the day of retirement. They find it painful to accept the finiteness of life; or they picture retirement years as filled with insufficient financial resources, boredom, poor health, and a lack of intellectual stimulation. For this group the failure to plan often results in the realization of their worst fears.

3. *Golden years* The third group, unfortunately, is small in number. They think and plan and enter retirement confidently and optimistically. This group usually finds that retirement is the high point in their lives.

Most of us spend 25 percent of our lives (our years in schools and colleges) preparing to be successful during the 50 percent of our lives devoted to active employment. Why shouldn't we also prepare for the other 25 percent of our lives that may well be spent in retirement?

Planning for life should continue in our retirement years. Usually those who are in their early retirement years avoid thinking about preparing themselves for the time when failing vigor may force changes in their life style. Does the journey into a more sedentary phase mean an end to the enjoyment of life? I don't think so, not if we have prepared ourselves properly.

Some of us may find our life's journey will include dependency during our final years. This can be a difficult period to contemplate (and with justification) because, all too frequently, senility and dependence on others for help in carrying out the bare essentials of everyday living characterizes this phase of life. In most cultures, however, senility is extremely rare. The prevalence of it in our society is partially due to health habits (the abuse of our cardio-vascular system) and to depression from the lack of purpose for life in retirement. Senility is sometimes a method of coping with depression. By careful planning we can delay, and probably eliminate, the dependency phase of our life.

Occupying the Summit offers something for almost everyone, but not all portions are equally applicable to every individual. Varied and unique abilities, interests, and financial situations require that each take an inventory of his or her status and make plans based upon individual circumstances. Those in their early working years may wish to spend limited time developing a brief and general plan and focus most of their time and energy on promoting skills to further their career.

Those a few years from retirement will want to develop a comprehensive plan which identifies specific actions and time allocated for accomplishments.

Those recently retired, or whose retirement is almost at hand, will want to recognize that the future will probably necessitate a change of life style and thus develop new interests and resources compatible with their abilities in later years.

Some may read this book and become concerned that they have waited too long in developing their plans. A positive plan at any stage of life can best assure that the remaining years are useful and enjoyable. Today is the first day of the rest of your life. Don't waste it.

> ROBERT W. SHAFFER
> Laguna Niguel, California

SECTION I: Financial Independence

Chapter 1—Facts 7
Chapter 2—Assumptions 17
Chapter 3—Your Plan — Preretirees 23
Chapter 4—Your Plan — Retirees 45
Chapter 5—Investment Alternatives and
                Strategies 59
Chapter 6—Contingency and Alternative
                Plans 97
Chapter 7—Monitoring Progress 105

Chapter 1
Facts

Facts

DETERMINING YOUR FINANCIAL STATUS

The material in this section helps you develop a financial plan to assure adequate financial resources during retirement. Section II covers planning needed so that your life will have a purpose after retirement. Section III outlines planning required to enjoy good health during your later years.

Work sheets for you to complete appear in the appendix. Their numbering system correlates to the section and chapter in which they are discussed. For example, WS-I.2.1 designates (WS work sheet) (I. first section) (2. second chapter) (1. first work sheet). A second work sheet for the same section and chapter would be labeled WS-I.2.2.

In preparing your financial plan, you first develop facts to find out where you are at present. You next determine where you want to go. You then develop a plan for proceeding from where you are (an accounting of your present financial resources) to where you want to go (to have sufficient income to live your desired life style during retirement years).

Net Worth Statement

Your first task is to prepare a net worth statement. Developing a net worth statement involves determining what you own, what you owe, and how much more you own than owe. Review and become familiar with WS-I.1.1. Be conservative in evaluating the worth of your car, household furnishings, clothing, etc. List their resale value, rather than the amount you paid for them.

Those who work for a salary or wages and are covered by a pension often overlook what a valuable asset their pension represents. This is especially true if the employer contributes the total funding for the pension. A simple way to estimate the equivalent asset value of your pension is to determine the investment required to produce the income you can expect from your pension. Most companies provide an employee handbook that gives the information necessary to compute pension benefits. Use the amount of the pension earned to date. Even if you change jobs, provided you have been employed by your present employer for a specified time (usually ten years), you will receive a pension sometime in the future (usually age 65).

The contribution your employer makes toward funding your pension is as much a part of your annual income as is the money in your paycheck. The difference is that the employer's contribution is not presently available. Those receiving wages and salaries often compare their incomes to self-employed professionals. You may appreciate your job more when you realize the amount of savings you would have to accumulate to provide the same income as your pension will provide upon your retirement.

You can easily determine the equivalent asset value of your pension. Let's say that you ascertain that you have presently earned an annual pension of $5,000 if you were 65 and retiring tomorrow. What amount of money would have to be invested in AAA corporate bonds in order to receive $5,000 a year in income? Assuming the bonds yield 10%, you would divide $5,000 by .10 and determine that the required investment would be $50,000. Complete WS-I.1.1 and calculate your net worth.

What Other Assets Are You Likely To Acquire?

Many of you anticipate inheritances from parents and/or other family members. You may wish to include such funds in your retirement planning. A word of caution: ill health on the part of your parents, continued inflation, and other misfortunes may erode much, or all, of your anticipated inheritance. It is better to make a conservative estimate than to anticipate receiving an inheritance and then finding it fails to materialize. Use your best judgement, and if you feel it is appropriate, show the amount of anticipated inheritance on WS-I.1.1.

Update your net worth statement annually. You may be surprised at the change from year to year. Hopefully, you won't be unpleasantly surprised and find it has decreased. If your net worth has decreased, then you have been living beyond your means and should take immediate corrective action. If the decline in asset value is allowed to continue, you are headed for serious financial difficulty and may even face insolvency and bankruptcy. Hopefully your statement will show an increase in net worth each year, and you will have proof that you are on your way to financial independence.

WHAT TYPE OF RETIREMENT DO YOU WANT?

Few individuals give this matter adequate thought. If you are going to retire to something, you should give serious thought as to what that something is going to be. Everyone, and especially retirees, needs the feeling that his or her life has a purpose.

Skill Inventory

WS-I.1.2 is provided for you and your spouse (if you are married) to list present skills. The reason for this inventory becomes evident as we progress in the planning process. The following questions should help stimulate your thinking:

> What skills did you acquire during your formal schooling?
> What courses did you take?
> In what extracurricular activities did you participate?
> To what organizations do you belong?
> What offices do you hold in these organizations?
> In what sports do you participate?
> What skills have you acquired on your job?
> How are you earning your living?
> What company courses have you taken?

Mission

During your active working years, you undoubtedly have a mission that is pretty well understood. You may feel it is to provide for the economic needs of your family, to give love and direction to your children, and to be a good spouse. The retiree may have a more difficult time identifying a mission during the retirement years. Many will find that identifying their mission is the most difficult part of retirement planning. Each must search within to determine what is right for him or her. We will address this subject in much more depth in Section II, Life With A Purpose. But you need to give some thought to the subject at this time so that you can arrive at a proposed retirement life style and then factor the costs into your financial planning.

Recreation Desired

Most look forward to retirement and the opportunity to spend more time at recreational activity. Whether it is golf, traveling, boating, etc., in all probability your plans will cost money. You should include these costs in your retirement expenses.

Intellectual and Social Needs

Intellectual stimulation and meaningful social interactions are important during retirement. During our working years these needs are, for the most part, met in the process of carrying out daily job responsibilities. This will change with retirement, and careful thought should be given as to how to satisfy these needs in the retirement years.

Those of you who are in your early working years may not want to spend extensive time in identifying the type of retirement you desire. You will have many years to come to grips with this matter. Those of you who are within a few years of retirement should resolve clearly in your mind what you want to retire TO.

If you are married, I suggest you and your spouse work independently and document desired retirement activities. After each is satisfied that he or she has identified and ranked personal desires, compare your lists. You may find you have compromises to work out. If the husband sees himself spending most of his time hunting and fishing while his wife perceives a retirement where they spend most of their time devoted to music and the arts, then obviously they must compromise if they intend to spend their retirement together, sharing common interests. After you have reached your compromises, complete WS-I.1.3.

WHERE DO YOU WANT TO LIVE?

Now you should have at least a general idea as to the type of retirement you desire. The next decision concerns where you want to live. Housing costs will probably be one of your major expenditures, and you will need a good estimate of these costs before you can start your financial planning. To estimate housing costs, you must first answer some questions.

Should You Remain In Your Present Home?

Prepare a list of advantages and disadvantages to remaining in your present home, similar to the following:

    Advantages
        Continue present friendships
        Remain close to relatives
        You like the community

Facts

You feel comfortable with the present services (doctor, dentist, attorney, etc.)

Disadvantages

Present unit too small

Community not suited to retirement

Climate

Present unit too large and/or expensive to maintain

Retirement requires adjustment. Those of you who have moved to new communities realize that moving, by itself, requires many adjustments and can be stressful. Making new friends, adjusting to a different climate, and finding new sources of services (doctors, etc.) can be difficult. So there are many benefits to staying in your present location.

On the other hand, you may live at your present location because it is convenient for commuting. For many reasons, that location may not be appropriate for your retirement life style. In that case, the best alternative may be to move. If your decision is to stay where you are, your work on this subject is completed. If your decision is to move, you have to decide where you plan to move.

How Do You Select a Retirement Location?

Some of the factors you should consider are

Climate

Ease of shopping

Medical facilities

Employment opportunities

Retirement or adult-only community

Availability of cultural amenities and educational facilities

Let's review these considerations. If you select a location that has a significant seasonal change, you may find yourself unhappy during part of each year. If you visualize an active life style upon retirement, then the cold, snow, and ice of winter can be very confining. On the other hand, you may have visited Arizona in the winter and become enthralled with the climate; but how about summer with average daytime temperatures over 100 degrees? How do you react to rain, gray overcast days, or fog? If you have had indoor employment, you may have had little concern for climate because your automobile and your working and living environments have had facilities to moderate the elements. You may find you will change your perception of a good climate after your retirement. You may believe your ideal retirement location is a remote acreage where you can grow some of your food, raise a few cattle, and get away from the urban rat race. Have you thought about the need for intellectual stimulation and the need for the availability of medical facilities in an emergency? You may find that you would like to have part-time employment upon retirement, either to supplement your income or to give your life a sense of purpose. Will your selected location give you an opportunity to engage in part-time work?

How do you feel about a retirement community? Do you want friends with a variety of ages and interests? Unfortunately, many retired people have narrow interests and tend to converse about their aches and pains, their latest trip, and how the country is going to the dogs. To surround yourself with this type of companions can be depressing.

On the other hand, if you live in a community with mixed age groups, you may find yourself living next door to Dennis the Menace. How about transportation? Failing health may necessitate that you relinquish your driving permit, leaving you without any form of transportation. Probably, there is no perfect location for you. But you can make the choice that has the most benefits and the fewest drawbacks.

Again, if you have several years until retirement, you have time to refine your thinking; but you should make a preliminary decision in order to estimate your retirement living costs.

What Type of Housing Do You Want?

Consider the many options for housing.

An individual home
A condominium or cooperative apartment
A mobile home
An apartment
A principal home and a second home

Many people get a great deal of satisfaction from taking care of a yard. The gratification received from beautifying their surroundings, as well as from the physical activity, contributes to their sense of well being. Many (including those who had little time for yard work during their active employment years) find the opportunity to engage in this activity rewarding. Others look forward to a life of freedom from the demands of yard maintenance. Which type are you?

Make a preliminary determination as to the type of housing you would like to occupy upon retirement. Some of the considerations include

Size
Proper layout or floor plan
Safety features
Energy requirements

You have all heard the complaint credited to the wife of a recently retired individual: "I now have twice as much husband and half the income." Those of you yet to retire probably find this lament amusing. For many retired couples, however, it has a bitter ring of truth. Two people in the space formerly occupied by one for most of the day can lead to problems. Most of us need space. We need a place of our own where we can get away by ourselves for part of the time to pursue our individual interests.

If your retirement plans include time spent on hobbies, perhaps your retirement home should include space dedicated to your hobby. On the other hand, too much space can become a burden. It can be difficult to clean and expensive to heat and cool.

Envision the life style you desire and try to define the ideal unit. How many spare bedrooms, if any, do you want? Do you plan to entertain extensively? If so, do you want a formal dining room? How about a den? What size living room? What facilities for hobbies? What size garage? Depending on climate, what are the requirements for energy, and what energy-saving provisions do you want in your home? As we grow older, stairs, bathtubs, etc., become more of a hazard because of potential injuries from falls. What safety features do you wish to have incorporated into your unit?

If you have decided that your present home is your retirement location, you know what your housing costs will be. If you have decided to move, you should estimate the costs associated with your new home. If the past is any indicator of the future, you can predict the price of housing will increase. But then, if you own (or are buying) your present home, it will also increase in value. Let us assume that the costs of your retirement home and your present home will remain relative and not consider the effects of inflation at this time. The logic of this assumption will become apparent when you prepare your financial plan.

COMMITTING YOUR IDEAS TO PAPER

Turn to WS-I.1.4. The first question is "What is your present home worth?" Use community resources to determine the answer. Perhaps a neighbor has sold his home recently, or you may have to ask a real estate person familiar with homes in your neighborhood. Also, determine the price of the lot. You may be surprised at what it is worth. A large part of the increase in the value of most homes has been in the cost of the land. Subtract the lot value from the cost of the unit, and you arrive at the value of the house without the lot. Next, how many square feet does your house have? Use the square feet of the living area and do not include the garage, patios, etc. By dividing the value of the house by the square footage, you can determine the value per square foot. You are now ready to make an educated guess as to the costs of your retirement dream home.

Estimate the number of square feet you desire in your retirement unit. Then determine what the square-foot cost is for housing in the community to which you plan to move. This may take some doing. If you know, or can determine, the cost of homes in the new community and the value of the lots, you can compute the cost in the same manner as you did for your present unit. If not, a letter to the chamber of commerce in the distant community, an inquiry to a nation-wide realtor, or perhaps a visit to the community may provide the answer. You can now multiply the cost per square foot by the desired square footage to estimate the cost of the retirement home you are considering.

Next, determine the price of the lot. The big difference in the cost of homes of similar size is largely due to the lot price. If you desire a home on the ocean, you will find the lot price much more expensive than an inland location. If you find that such a location will price the home beyond your means, you may wish to rethink where you want to live. Golf course lots are also expensive.

Add the lot price to the computed cost of the dwelling unit, and you will have a good estimate of the cost of your retirement home. You should now complete the balance of WS-I.1.4.

Assume you will take the existing equity in your present home and use it as a down payment on your retirement unit. Take the current mortgage interest cost and apply it to the amount of the mortgage, and you will have an estimate of the annual mortgage expense for your retirement home. You will be using this estimate when you begin preparing your Financial Plan in Chapter 3.

Chapter 2

Assumptions

Assumptions

Chapter 1 dealt with facts. This chapter covers the assumptions you need to make and include in your financial planning. Planning requires an input of both facts and assumptions. An assumption is a projection of future events. The only thing we know about the future is that it will not materialize as we predict. Thus you might ask, "Why make assumptions?" The answer is that we need them in the planning process. You must monitor your assumptions as time progresses, and if you find that they remain valid, you know your plan is still viable. If one or more of your assumptions change, you must revise your plan. Let's look at the assumptions you are being asked to make.

INFLATION

Inflation is a major concern for the majority of retirees. They are faced with increasing living costs that must somehow be met with a fixed income. So, anticipate that inflation must be a key ingredient in any retirement planning. No one knows what the inflation rate will be in the future. As this is being written, inflation is at its lowest level for years. Some economists are predicting a depression with "disinflation." Others see continued low inflation with a weak economic recovery. Still others predict a return to double-digit inflation because of our huge national-budget deficits. If economic scholars can't agree on future inflation rates, isn't it ridiculous for you to try to make such a prediction? Rather than making a prediction, however you will be making an assumption. If it subsequently appears that the average inflation rate is at, or below, your assumed rate, your financial plan is still valid. If inflation exceeds your assumed rate, you will need to rework your plan. Perhaps it would be of help to review past inflation rates.

PERIOD	INFLATION RATE
The 50s	2.0%
The 60s	2.3%
First Half of 70s	6.1%
Second Half of 70s	13.7%
1980 & 1981	12.0% +
1982 to 1989	4.0% +

Make your long-term inflation assumption and enter your figure on WS-I.2.1.

EARNINGS ON INVESTMENTS

A good basic rule is: For the lowest risk investments, money is worth three percent plus the anticipated long-term inflation rate. As the risk increases, the expected return increases by an amount commensurate with the risk.

Let's take an example. Corporate AAA bonds represent a long-term investment with a minimum risk. If the bonds are selling at face value, with a return of 11 percent, then it can be said that investors are anticipating an 8 percent long-term inflation rate. Bonds rated single A are deemed by bond-rating specialists to have more risk and would probably be yielding 11.25 percent to 11.5 percent. If you are willing to take the risk of loaning money on a second trust deed, you might receive a return of 18 percent on your invested funds. So, you see, once you have made your assumption on the rate of inflation, you have only to decide what risk you are willing to take on your invested funds, and you have a good assumption as to the return you will receive on your savings. Show your assumed return on low-risk investments on WS-I.2.1.

WHERE ARE YOU IN YOUR CAREER PROGRESSION?

This also is a difficult assumption to make, primarily because we all want to feel that we will continue to move up in the organization and receive many promotions. If you have been progressing up the corporate ladder and have every reason to anticipate further promotions, you may want to assume you will receive one, or more, promotions before your retirement. If you are in business for yourself or are in a profession, you should also make an assumption as to your future earnings in constant dollars. I would urge a conservative outlook as to your assumed earnings. Then if your future earnings are more than your assumed earnings, you will find yourself better off financially than you anticipated as retirement approaches. If, however, you overestimate your income, you will find yourself approaching, or at, retirement with less funds than you anticipated. This can be troublesome since you will have to reduce your anticipated style of living in your retirement years or delay your retirement. List your assumption as to your career progression on WS-I.2.1.

HOW LONG DO YOU WANT TO WORK?

Most people now have the opportunity to work at least until the age of 70, and for many there is no mandatory retirement age. So, for most, the question is no longer "When do I have to retire?" but rather "When do I want to retire?" This is progress. However, some will find that before they reach mandatory retirement, they would like to be able to get away from the tensions and pressures associated with their job.

When you construct your retirement plan, you need to have in mind some date when you plan to take retirement. Again, I would suggest that you pick a realistic date: one that will allow you the possibility of an earlier date than the mandatory one. Then, if the pressures and demands of the job become excessive, you will have the option of retiring. Also, if health (or other than job-related reasons) should make an early retirement desirable, you would have built that flexibility into your plan. If you are in a profession or business for yourself, you have different options. Many professional persons are able to begin working fewer hours, with less intensity, as their career progresses. Also, some people who own their own businesses find that they can hire others to look after the business and can begin a more modest schedule as they grow older. There is no right or wrong answer to when you should retire. It is a highly personal decision. Note your assumption on WS-I.2.1.

LONGEVITY OUTLOOK

Another assumption you should make is how long you and (if you are married) your spouse can expect to live. If you are going to retire and expect your pension, Social Security benefits, and savings to provide for your retirement years, you must determine if they will last you and your spouse for as long as you will need them. If you assume that we will continue to have inflation, your living expenses will continue to increase after retirement. You are going to have to consider this unpleasant probability in your retirement planning.

But how can you make an assumption about your longevity? Most medical authorities will tell you that the primary contributor to a long and healthy life is to have ancestors who had long and healthy lives. In other words, what genes did you inherit? How long did your grandparents and your parents live, and what sort of health did they enjoy in their latter years? If they died in an accident or from some unnatural cause, their age at death should be discounted.

What we can do is alter our genetic age by our health habits. The dangers of smoking, overweight, and stress to our longevity and health are well known. It is suggested you make an appraisal of your ancestors' life span and then evaluate their life styles and health habits as compared to yours to estimate your genetic age. Then factor in more or fewer years in accordance with the information found on WS-I.2.1. Again an optimism about your longevity is suggested since you don't want to find you have exhausted your funds before the last years of your life.

INCREASE IN SOCIAL SECURITY BENEFITS

At present, Social Security benefits are indexed to inflation. The first of each year, the benefits are increased on the same percentage basis as the past year's inflation rate. There is current national debate on whether this should continue. The increase in benefits presently offsets at least a part of the increase in living costs caused by inflation. So an assumption is needed concerning the future policy of indexing Social Security benefits to inflation. Show your assumption on WS-I.2.1.

You have now determined the facts and made the assumptions necessary to prepare your financial plan.

Chapter 3 covers the suggested planning method for preretirees. On completion of the plan, they will know the amount of savings they will need at the time of retirement to enable them to live their desired life style throughout their years of retirement.

Chapter 4 outlines the suggested planning method to be used by retirees. The method is similar. The question that the retiree is concerned with, however, is "Will my investments allow me to sustain my desired life style throughout my period of retirement?" Or, in other words, How much is enough? It is suggested that retirees read through the material found in Chapter 3 before moving on to Chapter 4.

Chapter 3

Your Plan — Preretirees

Your Plan — Preretirees

The objective of a financial plan for preretirees is to assure that sufficient funds are available at retirement to support a desired life style throughout the rest of their lives.

This chapter is designed for those who have not yet retired. Chapter 4 is for those who have already retired.

Those who are eligible to receive a pension and/or Social Security benefits upon retirement can estimate the income they will receive from these sources. They can also project the costs of maintaining their desired life style after retirement. Subtracting their living costs from the above sources of income identifies the imbalance in their estimated retirement budget. They can then determine the level of savings required to fund that deficit over their planned years of retirement. Unfortunately, inflation will probably continue after retirement, and the costs of some goods and services consumed during retirement will continue to increase. In order to sustain a desired life style, additional savings will be needed to fund these increased costs.

By combining the savings required to fund the deficit with those required to cover the increased costs experienced during retirement, you can answer the earlier question, How much is enough? In other words, you will know the amount of savings needed by retirement to support your desired life style throughout your planned years of retirement.

The material in this chapter provides a method for preretirement financial planning. Each individual's set of circumstances is unique, and you may find that the method outlined will have to be altered to fit your particular circumstances. The format suggested is only one approach, and you should feel free to adopt any method that will provide an answer to the amount of savings required to support your needs and desires during retirement.

You will be asked to

- Estimate your income from your pension and Social Security benefits
- Arrive at your estimated retirement expenses
- Determine the income tax applicable to your pension and Social Security income
- Compute the amount of investments required to generate enough income to balance the first year of your retirement budget and the increase of costs caused by inflation.
- Determine the savings required to provide sufficient investments at retirement.

PENSION INCOME

As was discussed in Chapter 1, most pension plans have a formula for determining the amount of pension due you upon retirement. The number of years of service to the employer and the level of salary obtained are usually parts of the formula. The number of years of service at the time of retirement can be estimated. The level of salary at the time of retirement is more difficult to determine because the amount of future salary adjustments is unknown.

If you will accept the premise that most individuals have reached their ultimate level in the organization by mid-career (probably sometime around 50 to 60), you can use this assumption in your planning method. Future salary increases, even though probably termed merit, will largely be determined by the future rates of inflation. It follows that the periodic increases, less the additional income tax liability associated with the raise, will sustain a constant purchasing power between the present and the time of your retirement.

If you believe you will receive one or more promotions, or your increases will be larger than the amount required to maintain your purchasing power, you may use that assumption in the pension formula.

By using your current salary (and, if you choose, any promotional increases expected) and the years of service at the time of retirement in the pension formula, you can arrive at the value of your future pension in today's dollars.

SOCIAL SECURITY BENEFITS

The future of Social Security is clouded. The change in the percentage receiving benefits to the percentage paying Social

Security taxes has changed significantly since its inception. Benefits have been expanded far beyond the intent of the original draftees of the program. Indexing the benefits to inflation has substantially increased the costs of the program. All of these factors, and more, have raised questions as to the future of the program. In all probability the program will continue, and individuals in their forties and fifties can count on receiving benefits at the time of their retirement.

The formula used to determine the level of benefits due an individual is complex. A visit or a call to your local Social Security office will enable you to obtain material that explains how benefits are computed.

One of the inputs into the formula is your past years' earning bases. The bases are determined by the portion of your earnings on which you paid Social Security taxes. In 1954 it was $3,600. The base has increased substantially in recent years. For example, in 1984 it was $37,800. The Social Security Administration also establishes an annual index factor which is applied to the earnings base. The sum of each year's earnings base, times the index factor applicable to that year, provides a total indexed earnings. The maximum number of years that apply is 35. Dividing the total indexed earnings by 35 and then by 12 gives the average indexed monthly earnings. This answer is used in a formula. The formula for 1983 and 1984 follows:

	1983	1984	
90% of the first	$ 254	$ 267	$_____
32% of the next	1,274	1,345	$_____
15% of the remaining	_____	_____	$_____
		Total	$_____

Unless the policies of the Social Security Administration change drastically, it would appear that future benefits will increase as indicated by the following points.

1. The earnings base will probably increase in future years.
2. In the past, the index factors have increased with each passing year and thus the total indexed earnings for each year is increased.
3. The amount to which the 90 percent and 32 percent is applied increases as indicated in the above example.

Also, unless the benefit is increased, those already retired would be receiving higher benefits than an individual just planning to retire, since the retiree's benefits are indexed to inflation.

In your planning process it appears reasonable to assume that you will receive Social Security benefits and that they will be higher than those you would currently receive if you had maximum coverage and had reached the age of 65. However, again it is suggested you assume this increase (together with the increase in your pension benefits) will offset your increased cost of living between now and the time you retire.

Your income from your pension and Social Security benefits will be more at the time of your retirement than the figures arrived at by using the above assumptions. But so will the retirement expenses you will incur in sustaining your desired life style. By using this assumption, you can predict whether you will have a surplus or a deficit in the first year of your retirement budget.

RETIREMENT LIVING COSTS

Your next task is to estimate your retirement expenses. First, prepare your current expense budget. Then you will prepare an estimated retirement budget.

Refer to WS-I.3.1, Column A. You may wish to add or delete the items shown, based upon your particular circumstances. If you have been using a budget, this should not be difficult. If you have not, let me suggest you start. It isn't as hard as you may think. The following are a few suggestions to simplify the task.

First, pay as many bills by check or credit card as possible. Caution: don't get in the habit of carrying a balance on your credit card account; pay up each month. This will give you an excellent record of most of your expenses and the type of expenditures you make. Keep a notebook at some convenient location and record daily cash expenditures. Then, once a month, using your bank and credit card statements and the log of your cash expenditures, categorize and total that month's expenditures.

At this time, do the best you can at estimating your present annual expenditures. A review of your check stubs, utility bills, etc., should enable you to make a fairly accurate estimate of your annual expenses. Complete Column A, of WS-I.3.1.

Next ask yourself, "If I/we were to retire tomorrow, what type of retirement activities would I/we engage in, and how would I/we spend our money?" It may be helpful to review WS-1.1.4 prepared in Chapter 1.

I will point out some of the things you may wish to consider. Record your answers on WS-I.3.1, Column B.

Housing

You have considered your housing preferences and the cost of your retirement housing. Use your present costs for taxes, insurance, and utilities, and then adjust for the difference in climate, location, etc., and arrive at an estimate for these costs. If you are moving to a new community, you can review the data compiled by the U. S. Bureau of Statistics related to comparative living costs for various cities and sections of the country. You can obtain this information by a visit to your local library.

Food

After you have arrived at your present expenditures for food, estimate the amount you would spend if retired. If you now have children at home, they will probably be gone when you retire, and your food expenditures could be considerably less. Will you dine out more or less after you retire? You may be spending a sizeable amount today for lunches which might decrease after retirement.

Clothing

The amount you presently spend on clothes, as well as cleaning, should decrease after you retire.

Transportation

Transportation costs should be considerably less, especially if you have an expensive commute to work. You may elect to have only one automobile whereas you have two today. Gas consumption could be less, and automobile maintenance costs would decrease with less usage.

Recreation

You are probably looking forward to retirement so you can spend more time at recreational activities. Many look forward to retirement as an opportunity to do more traveling. If you can afford it, it would be a shame not to include these activities, and the necessary funds, in your retirement plans. Arrive at the costs for you and your spouse to participate in hobbies, sports, travel, etc., and include them in your retirement budget.

Life Insurance

You may have life insurance to provide for your family in the event of your death. You may find those needs will be different by the time you retire. Your spouse may, at that time, be protected by income from investments and joint survivor provisions of your pension, and the needs for insurance will be changed or eliminated.

Medical Expenses

These costs have escalated alarmingly during the past few years and give every indication of continuing to increase in the future. Does your company provide medical and dental coverage for their retirees? If so, what percentage of the costs do they cover? Medicare will provide some coverage when you reach 65. Medical costs vary widely by region. Try to obtain information on the relative costs in the community in which you plan to retire.

Contributions To Charity

You will probably want to allocate some of your retirement income to gifts to your church, favorite charity, or a philanthropic organization.

Gifts

Christmas, birthdays, anniversaries, and other gift-giving occasions still occur after retirement. You may wish to scale down the amount you are presently spending for such items.

Miscellaneous And Contingency

Many small day-to-day expenditures are difficult to categorize in a budget. Also, unplanned expenditures occur from time to time. The amounts can be substantial unless you have good control over impulse buying. On the other hand, it is nice to have a budgeted amount that will allow you to make occasional purchases without destroying your budget. If you have difficulty in arriving at a figure, I suggest you budget five percent of your gross income.

Total the expenditures in Column B of WS-I.3.1 for an estimate of your retirement expenses in today's dollars. Next, separate these expenses into those that will increase because of inflation after retirement and those that will not. We will label these inflation-impacted and inflation-free expenses.

Inflation-Free Expenses

Inflation-free expenses are those that will not increase over time as the result of inflation. Examples are a fixed-rate mortgage and life insurance premiums. You may elect to treat other budget items as inflation free, even though they will be impacted by inflation. For example, you may decide to budget $5,000 for an annual vacation and spend only that amount each year of your retirement. This will result in more modest trips as the years pass and the costs of vacations increase. Other examples might be amounts budgeted for gifts and charities.

Inflation-Impacted Expenses

After you have totaled your inflation-free expenses, consider all other expenses inflation impacted.

You now have an estimate of your retirement budget for the first year of retirement. This will be referred to as the base year of your retirement planning budget.

INCOME TAX ON PENSION AND SOCIAL SECURITY BENEFITS

The next category of expense you should estimate is the income tax applicable to your pension, and possibly, your Social Security benefits. You can do this by completing WS-I.3.2 and following the instructions.

You now have the information necessary to complete lines 1 through 10 of WS-I.3.3. Your income consists of your pension and Social Security benefits. Expenses are your inflation-free and inflation-impacted expenses plus the estimated income tax due on your estimated pension and Social Security benefits.

NOTE: Income from investments has not been included in your base-year budget. Remember the objective is to determine the amount of investments required to sustain your desired life style throughout retirement.

SAVINGS REQUIRED FOR RETIREMENT

You are now ready to determine the amount of savings required to sustain your desired life style throughout your estimated years of retirement. To accomplish this, use assumptions. In Chapter 2 you made the assumptions as to (1) the number of years until retirement, (2) the number of years of retirement, and (3) inflation expectations. This chapter presented the subject of Social Security benefit indexing to aid you in making an assumption as to this probability. Record these assumptions on lines 23, 24, 25, and 26 of WS-I.3.3.

AFTER-TAX EARNINGS ON INVESTMENTS

The remaining two assumptions needed are an estimate of the after-tax earnings on your investments, before and after you retire. To accomplish this, you determine your present marginal tax rate and estimate your marginal tax rate after retirement. Your marginal tax rate is the highest tax rate applicable to your investment income. The following example will assist you in determining the marginal tax rate applicable to your investments.

Marginal Tax Rate

Suppose your latest Federal Income Tax Return (1987) shows the following:

Taxable income (line 36 form 1040) $35,234

The Tax Table for Married Filing Jointly, (page 37) includes the following tax bracket:

28,000   45,000   4,080 + 28%   28,000

Your marginal tax bracket is 28%

Use the same procedure for your state income tax return to determine your state marginal tax rate.

As this is being written, your state income tax is used as a deduction on your federal return. Your combined marginal tax rate is your federal marginal tax rate plus one-half your state marginal tax rate.

Your after-tax earnings can be computed by using the following formula:

After-Tax Earnings = Before-Tax Earnings multiplied by
(1 − Combined Marginal Tax Rate)
Example:
Before-Tax Earnings = 8%
Combined Marginal Tax Rate = 31%
.08 × (1 − .31) = .0552 or 5.52%

In this example your after-tax earnings are 5.52 percent.

Since your income will probably be less after you retire, it follows that your income taxes and your marginal tax rate will also be lower. And after-tax earnings on your investments should be more. On WS-I.3.2 you computed the estimated tax on your pension and

Your Plan — Preretirees

Social Security benefits. From this information you can estimate your after-retirement combined marginal tax rate and your after-tax earnings on your investments.

Show your assumptions of after-tax earnings on lines 28 and 29 of WS-I.3.3.

Before completing the rest of WS-I.3.3, you may wish to turn to Exhibit 2 at the end of this chapter. It is an example of how a preretiree can use this material to prepare a financial plan.

INVESTMENTS REQUIRED

Next turn to WS-I.3.3, page 2. Using your assumptions, fill in the column COORDINATES. Determine the appropriate FACTORS by using the tables found in Exhibit 1 at the end of this chapter. Copy the factor obtained on the proper line on WS-I.3.3, page 1, per the instructions. Complete the mathematical calculations called for on WS-I.3.3, lines 11 through 22, and you have the answers to

- Total investment required (How much is enough?)
- Annual savings required between now and retirement to accumulate the required investments

ANALYSIS OF FINANCIAL PLAN FOR RETIREMENT

Let's analyze the meaning of the information shown on WS-I.3.3.

First, look at the base-year retirement budget. If a deficit is projected for the base-year budget, the amount of investments required to fund the deficit is determined by computing an equivalent annuity. This will provide an annual income equal to the annual deficit over the planning period.

The amount of income you will need is after-tax income, so after-tax earning returns were used.

If you have the amount of investments shown to be required on line 11 of WS-I.3.3, and you are willing to use the principal and income each year, as required to balance your base-year budget, then your budget would remain in balance over the planning period.

However, inflation will cause your inflation-impacted expenses to increase each year of the planning period. The method we will use to deal with this problem will be discussed shortly.

If a base-year surplus is predicted, the annuity principle is again used, but in this case the computed amount is considered a contribution to the required investment.

This contribution is shown on line 17 of WS-I.3.3.

Your budget would now be in balance, if it were not for the increased costs of your inflation-impacted expenses over the years between the base year and the last year of the planning period. Few individuals truly understand the impact of inflation on their living expenses. One needs only to recall the price of a loaf of bread, an automobile, or a visit to a doctor 15 or 20 years ago to comprehend the devastating effect of inflation on a budget. Until retirement you probably received periodic wage increases that offset these increased costs. Retirees usually cannot expect such increases in their pensions.

Inflation

To better understand the forces of inflation, consider what would happen to $20,000 of expenses over a 20-year period at various rates of inflation:

Inflation Rate	Inflation-Impacted Expenses	
	Base Yr.	Yr. 20
4%	$20,000	$ 43,000
6%	20,000	64,143
8%	20,000	93,219
10%	20,000	134,550
12%	20,000	192,926

The next task is to determine the amount of investments required to purchase the same goods and services, in each year of the planning period, as you assumed you would need in the base year. In the above example, at a six-percent inflation rate, you would need $44,143 of additional funds to make the same purchases in year 20 as you did in the base year [$64,143 minus $20,000]. The amount required will be small the first years [Year 1 only $1,200 − $20,000 × .06 = $1,200].

Line 13 on WS-I.3.3 shows the amount of investment required to sustain your purchasing power for the goods and services identified in your inflation-impacted expenses, provided:

- You use the principal and interest as required and
- Your after-tax earnings on investments equals your assumed inflation rate.

The investment required to fund impacted expenses is computed assuming that after-tax earnings equal the inflation rate. If the after-

Your Plan — Preretirees 35

tax earnings are more than the inflation rate, then fewer investments will be required. If the after-tax earnings are less than the inflation rate, then more investments will be required. Line 14 adjusts line 13 in accordance with your assumptions on after-tax earnings and inflation.

If you assumed that Social Security benefits will continue to be indexed at, or less than, the inflation rate, the increase in benefits will at least partially offset the increase in living costs. Line 15 of WS-I.3.3 gives the value of this offset.

Adding line 11 (investment required to fund base-year deficit) to or subtracting line 17 (contribution of base-year surplus) from line 16 determines the total investment required.

The portion of WS-I.3.3 labeled YOUR PLAN considers your existing investments and identifies the annual savings required to assure sufficient funds upon retirement to sustain your desired life style through the planning period.

Line 19 asks for your existing investments. You identified the amount when you computed your net worth in Chapter 1. Use the income-producing assets, less any loans you have incurred in obtaining these assets.

Line 20 forecasts the value of these investments at the time of your retirement by using your assumptions of years until retirement and after-tax earnings before retirement.

Line 21 compares the investments required to the investments you forecast having by the time you retire.

Line 22 shows the annual savings required each year between the present and the time you plan to retire if a shortage of existing investments is indicated on line 21.

The Savings Program

The question you must now answer is, Can I realistically expect to make the annual savings required? If you believe you can, you are ready to move to Chapter 5, Investment Alternatives And Strategies.

If you believe it impossible to acquire the amount of capital required, you have several alternatives:

1. You can generate more income before retirement, after retirement, or both. The chapter on Investment Alternatives and Strategies and the chapter on Contingency and Alternative Plans offer suggestions as to how this may be accomplished.

2. You can reduce your living costs before retirement, after retirement, or both. The chapter on Contingency and Alternative Plans should be of help on how this may be accomplished.
3. You can reduce income taxes before or after retirement, or both, to increase your after-tax earnings. The chapter on Investment Alternatives and Strategies provides ideas as to how this might be accomplished.

Living With The Assumptions

Those individuals many years from retirement probably have qualms about some of the figures and assumptions used in their plan. The uncertainty as to their actual pension and Social Security benefits, the sketchy concept of the life style desired, and doubts as to future economic climates and inflation rates cause them to lack confidence in their plan. The accuracy of their projections and assumptions is not as important as the realization that they will probably need savings to balance their retirement budget. The important thing for this group is to put savings high on the priority of how they handle their disposable income.

As retirement nears, it is possible to arrive at figures for use in the plan with much more accuracy. Chapter 7 of this section, Monitoring Progress, suggests an annual update of the plan. Thus each plan becomes more factual as you near your retirement.

The next chapter is directed to those individuals who are already retired. I suggest preretirees read through the material, since it will give insight into some of the concerns encountered in retirement. It also demonstrates how financial planning can be utilized by those already retired.

Chapter 5 of this section covers investment alternatives and strategies. Your skills as an investor greatly influence your ability to obtain and maintain a retirement with financial security. Unfortunately, many individuals are so preoccupied with the demands of their job that they spend little time in acquiring the knowledge and skill necessary to build their investment portfolio. A static investment strategy applied to a fluctuating economic environment will probably cause a serious erosion of savings dollars and/or purchasing power.

EXHIBIT 1, PAGE 1

TABLE A
ANNUITY
INTERESTS

YEARS	4%	6%	8%	10%	12%
5	.225	.237	.250	.264	.277
10	.123	.136	.149	.163	.178
15	.090	.103	.117	.131	.147
20	.074	.087	.102	.117	.134
25	.064	.078	.094	.110	.127
30	.058	.073	.089	.106	.124

If an investment earns _____ % and _____ equal payments of principal and interest are withdrawn each year, then _____ of the original investment can be withdrawn annually.

TABLE B
FUTURE VALUE
INTEREST OR INFLATION

YEARS	4%	6%	8%	10%	12%
5	1.22	1.34	1.47	1.61	1.76
10	1.48	1.79	2.16	2.59	3.11
15	1.80	2.40	3.17	4.18	5.47
20	2.19	3.21	4.66	6.73	9.65
25	2.67	4.29	6.85	10.83	17.00
30	3.24	5.74	10.06	17.45	29.96

If the annual rate of inflation (or annual earnings on an investment) is _____ % in _____ years, the cost of living (or value of the investment) will increase by a factor of _____ .

TABLE C
VALUE OF ANNUAL INVESTMENT COMPOUNDED
INTERESTS

YEARS	4%	6%	8%	10%	12%
5	5.42	5.64	5.87	6.11	6.35
10	12.00	13.18	14.49	15.94	17.55
15	20.02	23.28	27.15	31.77	37.28
20	29.78	36.79	46.76	57.27	72.05
25	41.65	54.86	73.11	98.35	133.33
30	56.08	79.06	113.21	164.49	241.33

An annual investment, if invested at _____ %, in _____ years will grow by a factor of _____ .

EXHIBIT 1, PAGE 2

LIFE STYLE ASSURANCE

TABLE D-1

YEARS OF RETIREMENT	ASSUMED INFLATION RATE DURING RETIREMENT WITH AFTER-TAX EARNINGS EQUAL TO INFLATION				
	4%	6%	8%	10%	12%
5	.37	.53	.69	.83	.96
10	1.56	2.20	2.75	3.24	3.67
15	3.44	4.71	5.76	6.63	7.37
20	5.87	7.84	9.40	10.64	11.63
25	8.75	11.45	13.47	15.02	16.22
30	12.02	15.41	17.84	19.63	20.98

TABLE D-2

AFTER-TAX EARNINGS GREATER THAN INFLATION RATE

	1%	2%	3%	4%	5%
5	.98	.96	.92	.91	.89
10	.94	.89	.84	.80	.75
15	.92	.84	.77	.71	.66
20	.89	.79	.71	.64	.58
25	.87	.75	.66	.58	.51
30	.84	.72	.61	.52	.45

TABLE D-3

AFTER-TAX EARNINGS LESS THAN INFLATION RATE

	1%	2%	3%	4%	5%
5	1.04	1.07	1.09	1.12	1.14
10	1.06	1.13	1.20	1.27	1.35
15	1.09	1.20	1.31	1.43	1.57
20	1.13	1.28	1.44	1.61	1.83
25	1.17	1.37	1.58	1.82	2.14
30	1.20	1.45	1.73	2.06	2.50

© Copyright 1986 by Robert W. Shaffer

WS-I.3.1

EXHIBIT 2, PAGE 1
PERSONAL EXPENSE BUDGET

Prepared for:
JOHN AND MARY DOE
Date: 8-8-88

	Current (A)	Cost Today If Retired (B)
HOUSING		
Mortgage Payment or Rent	$ 12,000	$ 12,000
Taxes and Insurance	1,200	1,200
Upkeep	1,000	800
Utilities	2,400	2,400
TOTAL HOUSING EXPENSE	$ 16,600	$ 16,600
FOOD		
Groceries & Misc.	$ 2,600	$ 2,600
Dining Out	2,000	2,000
TOTAL FOOD	$ 4,600	$ 3,600
CLOTHING		
New Clothes	$ 3,000	$ 1,500
Cleaning	600	200
TOTAL CLOTHING	$ 3,600	$ 1,700
TRANSPORTATION		
Car Payments & Insurance	$ 1,300	$ 1,000
Gas, Oil, & Maintenance	1,200	600
Other Transportation	500	none
TOTAL TRANSPORTATION	$ 3,000	$ 1,600
RECREATION		
Vacation & Travel	$ 1,000	$ 5,000
Other Recreation	1,200	3,000
TOTAL RECREATION	$ 2,200	$ 8,000
LIFE INSURANCE	$ 1,200	$ none
MEDICAL & MEDICAL INSURANCE	$ 1,200	$ 2,000
GIFTS & CHARITIES	$ 4,000	$ 3,000
MISCELLANEOUS EXPENSES	$ 4,000	$ 2,000
OTHER EXPENSES	$ 1,200	$ 1,200
TOTAL EXPENSES	$ 41,600	$ 39,500

INFL.-FREE EXPENSES $ 20,000
INFL.-IMPACTED EXPENSES $ 19,500

EXHIBIT 2, PAGE 2

WS-I.3.2
Page 1

INCOME TAX DUE ON PENSION

FEDERAL INCOME TAX (F.I.T.) DUE ON PENSION

(1) Estimated Pension in Today's Dollars $ 30,000
    (See note below)
(2) Itemized Deductions (Est. at time of retirement)   6,900
(3) Net (line 1 minus line 2)   23,040
(4) Personal Deductions   4,160
(5) Taxable Income from Pension only (L3 - L4)   18,880
(6) Tax (Use Tax Table)

  $ 1,811 plus 18% of ($ 18,880 minus $ 16,650)   2,212

CALIFORNIA STATE INCOME TAX (S.I.T.) DUE ON PENSION

(7) Estimated Pension in Today's Dollar $ 30,000
    (See note below)
(8) Itemized Deductions (Est. at time of retirement)   6,700
(9) Net (line 7 minus line 8)   23,300
(10) Tax (Use Tax Table)

  $ 320 plus 4% of ($ 23,300 minus $ 20,140)   446
(11) Personal Deductions   84
(12) Net Tax (line 10 minus line 11)   362

(13) TOTAL INCOME TAX DUE ON PENSION (L6 + L12) $ 2,574

NOTE: Itemized Deductions on Line 2 and Line 8 above would be the amount you would show on Line 26 of Schedule A of the Federal Return and Line 33 of Schedule NR A of the California State Return.

EXHIBIT 2, PAGE 3

WS-I.3.2
Page 2

FEDERAL INCOME TAX DUE ON SOCIAL SECURITY BENEFIT

(14) One-Half of Your Est. Annual Value
Soc. Sec. Bnft. in Today's Dollars
(See Note 1, next page) $ 5,000

(15) Est. Value of All Other Sources of Income
at Time of Retirement in Today's Dollars
(Include pension, investment income, etc.) 33,450
(See note 2, next page)

(16) Total Income (Line 14 + Line 15) 38,450

(17) Itemized Deductions (Est. at time of retirement) 6,960

(18) Personal Deductions 4,160

(19) Net Income (Line 15 minus Line 16 plus Line 17) 27,330

(20) Base Amount Above Which a Portion of Soc. Sec.
Benefit Is Taxable ($32,000 joint or $25,000
individual filing) 32,000

(21) Compare Line 19 with Line 20.
If Line 19 is less than Line 20   NO TAX IS DUE
If Line 19 is more than Line 20 show difference xxxx

(22) Taxable Social Security Benefit
(Line 21 times 50%) none

(23) Applicable Tax Rate (Line 6, page 1.) 18 %

(24) Federal Income Tax on Soc. Sec. Bnft.
(Line 22 times Line 24) none

(25) TOTAL INCOME TAX DUE ON PENSION
AND SOCIAL SECURITY BENEFIT
(ADD LINES 13 AND 24) $ 2,547
SHOW THE ABOVE AMOUNT ON WS-I.3.3, LINE 7.

EXHIBIT 2, PAGE 4

WS-I.3.2
Page 3

NOTE 1. If you had paid the maximum Social Security tax each year and reached the age of 65 in 1984, you would be entitled to a maximum benefit of $703 per month or $8,436 annually. If you chose to receive your benefit at 62, the amount you would be entitled to receive would be 80% of the maximum benefit or $6,748. A spouse at age 65 would be entitled to 50% of the primary benefit. If you have paid less than the maximum Social Security tax in the past or you will have less than 35 years of coverage by the time you retire, a visit to the local Social Security office will enable you to obtain literature that will assist you in estimating your future benefit stated in the value of today's dollars.

NOTE 2. A portion of your Social Security benefit may be subject to Federal Income tax if your income from your pension, investment income (including tax free income) and one-half of your Social Security benefit exceeds $25,000 for an individual or $32,000 for those filing jointly. In order to estimate whether a portion of your Social Security benefit will be taxable, it will be necessary for you to make an estimate of the amount of income you will receive from investments at the time of your retirement.

EXHIBIT 2, PAGE 5

WS-I.3.3
Page 1

FINANCIAL PLAN
FOR RETIREMENT

Name JOHN AND MARY DOE   Date 9-5-88

Line	RETIREMENT BUDGET			Base Year
1.	INCOME			
2.	Pension			$ 30,000
3.	Soc. Sec.			10,000
4.	Total Income	L2 + L3		40,000
5.	EXPENSE			
6.	Inflation Free			20,000
7.	Inc. Tx. (Pens. & Soc. Sec.)			2,574
8.	Inflation-Impacted			19,500
9.	Total Expense	L6 + L7 + L8		42,074
10.	DEFICIT OR SURPLUS	L4 - L9		$ (2,074)
	INVESTMENT REQUIRED		Factor(1)	
11.	To Cover First-Year Deficit	L10/factor	.102	$ 20,333
12.	To Cover Incr. Infl.-Impacted Exp.			
13.	Impacted Expense Only	L8 x factor	7.84	152,880
14.	If Aft-Tx Earn is not = Infl.	L13 x factor	.79	120,775
15.	Soc. Sec. Contribution	L3 x factor	5.87	58,700
16.	Net Required	L14 - L15		62,075
17.	First-Year Surplus Contribution	L10/factor		(xxxxx)
18.	TOTAL INVESTMENT REQUIRED	L16 + L11 or L16 - L17		82,408
	YOUR PLAN			
19.	Existing Investments			$ 25,000
20.	Investments at Time of Retirement	L19 x factor	1.98	49,500
21.	Excess (Shortage) of Investments	L20 - L18		32,908
22.	Annual Svgs. Req. If Shortage	L21/factor	13.84	$ 2,378

(1) See Page 2 For Factors

	ASSUMPTIONS		
23.	Years Until Retirement	10	yrs.
24.	Years of Retirement	20	yrs.
25.	Inflation Expectations	6	%
26.	% Annual Incr. in Soc. Sec.	4	%
27.	After-Tax Earnings on Invest.		
28.	Before Retirement	7	%
29.	After Retirement	8	%

(c) Copyright 1986 by Robert W. Shaffer

WS-I.3.3
Page 2

INSTRUCTIONS FOR COMPLETING WS-I.3.3

STEP 1. Obtain the dollar amounts to be shown on Lines 2, 3, 6, 7, 8 and 19 from previously completed work sheets. List your assumptions on Lines 23 through 29.

STEP 2. Use your assumptions to fill in the blanks under the column labeled COORDINATES on the supplemental work sheet below. Find the value of the factors by using the coordinates and the table in Exhibit 1 found at the end of Chapter 3, Section 1. Show the factor on the proper line on WS-I.3.3, Page 1.

SUPPLEMENTAL WORK SHEET

	COORDINATES		TABLE	FACTOR	SHOW ON LINE OF WS-I.3.3, PAGE 1
% Aft-Tx Earn Aft Retir.	Yrs. of Ret.				
__8__ %	__20__ Yrs.	A		__.102__	11 (If 1st Yr Deficit)
					17 (If 1st Yr Surplus)
% Inflation	Yrs. of Ret.				
__6__ %	__20__ Yrs.		D-1	__7.84__	13
% S.S. Incr.	Yrs. of Ret.				
__4__ %	__20__ Yrs.		D-1	__5.87__	15

AFT-TX EARN AFT RET (_8_%) minus INFL ASSUMPTION (_6_%) = _2_%
(DIFFERENCE)

IF DIFFERENCE IS ZERO
The Factor Is   1.0   14

IF DIFFERENCE MORE THAN ZERO
More By:	Yrs. of Ret.				
__2__ %	__20__ yrs.		D-2	__.79__	14

IF THE DIFFERENCE IS LESS THAN ZERO
Less By:	Yrs. of Ret.				
xx %	___ yrs.		D-3	xxx	14

% Aft-Tx Earn Before Ret.	Yrs. Until Retirement				
__7__ %	__10__ yrs.	B		__1.98__	20
% Aft-Tx Earn Before Ret.	Yrs. Until Retirement				
__7__ %	__10__ yrs.	C		__13.84__	22

STEP 3. Complete the mathematical calculations called for in the instructions on WS-I.3.3, Page 1.

Chapter 4

Your Plan — Retirees

Your Plan — Retirees

Retirees, and those people anticipating retirement in the near future, are usually concerned about the effects of inflation on their future ability to maintain an acceptable life style. They often have made little or no effort to analyze their financial situation and indeed do not know how to make such an evaluation. The unknown creates concern and anxiety, preventing them from enjoying their golden years.

This concern is usually not necessary. We tend to fear the unknown. Once the facts are known, we can generally take action to calm our fears.

TYPICAL RETIREMENT SITUATIONS

The following are some of the typical situations in which retirees find themselves and their reactions to their perceived situation:

Limited Income — Limited Consumption

Individuals in this category have often been retired for several years. Many do not live on a budget and have only a vague awareness of how they spend their income. Conservative in their investment policy, most believe that their savings are prudently invested. Each year inflation increases the costs of goods and services. These retirees are frightened and resentful as they see their savings gradually being consumed by current living costs.

Sufficient Income — Phobic Underconsumption

Individuals in this category have a phobia either about the present rate of inflation or about what they fear they may experience in the future. Their current income is significantly greater than their expenses. Their goal in life is to increase the size of their investments as a hedge against possible future expenses. Their present life is without joy, and they are apprehensive about the future. If one spouse fits this category while the other is an impulsive spender, they may be experiencing marital conflicts.

Sufficient Income — Erratic Consumption

People in this category tend to become impulsive spenders when anxious or depressed. Their purchase of nonessential items, such as clothing, jewelry, or gadgets, improves their sense of well-being. After the thrill of the purchase wears off, the good feeling is replaced by remorse. Thus their erratic pattern of consumption, which is influenced by their emotional state, has little relation to their needs. They find it difficult to prepare and live on a budget. Before retirement, their pattern of consumption caused little concern: they saved little and used credit frequently. However, with a fixed income, their erratic consumption pattern now threatens their future financial security.

Excellent Income — Conspicuous Consumption

The primary reason for the spending pattern of this group is to impress others. Many in this group had their ego massaged by corporate perks and/or their professional status prior to retirement. They still attempt to achieve their prior status by driving the right automobile, taking prestigious trips, and living in an expensive home. Their social conversation is carefully sprinkled with references to the size of their investment portfolio and their skill in investing. They fear inflation because it may limit the level of their conspicuous consumption and thus, as they perceive it, their status in the eyes of their associates. If the value of their investments increases they feel euphoric; however, a decline in the stock market will find them experiencing a loss of self-worth.

Most of us probably have difficulty identifying completely with any of the above types. Rather, we may sense that, in some ways, we relate to all of them.

PREPARING YOUR BASIC PLAN

The objective of this chapter is to help remove your apprehension about the future. Planning tools discussed should enable you to more effectively manage your financial resources.

The method suggested is similar to the one outlined for preretirees. Work sheets provided for the retiree's use are only slightly modified from those suggested for preretirees.

In some respects, financial planning for retirees is much simpler for retirees than it is for preretirees. Retirees know the respective amounts of their pension and Social Security benefits. They also know, or should know, their expenditures for the goods and services required to sustain their desired life style. They know the current amount of income tax due on their pension and Social Security benefits, and they know the current tax policy of the state and nation in which they reside. The retiree has the advantages of using many more "knowns" and fewer assumptions in their planning process.

However, the focus of their planning changes. Most preretirees question whether prior to retirement they will *be able to acquire* sufficient savings to enable them to sustain their desired life style throughout their retirement. The retiree's concern is whether *they own* sufficient investments to sustain their desired life style.

For married couples, it is very important that both partners participate in the financial planning. It is almost a certainty that eventually one will be left without the other. The transition will be much less traumatic if the one left participated in the planning process and fully understands their current economic situation and any actions recommended in the plan.

Let's see how a hypothetical couple, Dick and Jane, might go about their financial planning. But first let's get acquainted with them.

Dick and Jane

Dick and Jane retired five years ago. They moved from the Midwest to a retirement community near Tucson, Arizona. Dick had held several jobs before starting work for a large utility at the age of 35. He spent 30 years with the utility and advanced to the position of construction superintendent. He was making $32,000 at retirement at age 65. They receive a joint-survivor pension of $10,000 per year. Jane is the same age as Dick. Their combined Social Security benefits are $9,000 per year. After their two sons left home, Jane worked part-time at the local bank. She was not entitled to a pension. They had invested her income and Dick had participated in his company's stock purchase plan. As a result, at the time of their retirement, they had accumulated $80,000 of savings. They also had their home paid for. They sold their home when they moved to Arizona and paid cash for their retirement home. They realized a significant appreciation on their home in the Midwest and, taking advantage of the once-in-a-lifetime $100,000 exemption of the sale of their home, were able to pay cash for their retirement home and have $30,000 left over. This they combined with the $80,000 of savings and invested $110,000 in tax-free municipal bonds.

The time immediately after their retirement had been troublesome. Dick had become bored with all his leisure time, and Jane had missed the social contacts of her old friends and associates at the bank. But they finally evolved into a retirement life style that they both enjoyed. Both Dick and Jane played golf on an average of twice a week. They bowled in a mixed-couples league and played bridge several evenings a month with other couples in their retirement community. Dick served as a neighborhood commissioner for the local Boy Scout Council. Jane volunteered her services two mornings a week at the local hospital. Dick attended classes at the junior college and was presently taking a course in geology. They were active in their local church. They wished they lived closer to their children and grandchildren. Dick and Jane visited them once a year, usually over the Christmas holidays, and the children traveled to see them each year. They also participated in an Elderhostel program each year.

They felt their life had a purpose, and they were happy and contented in their retirement life style. With one exception. Every time they went to the grocery store, food prices seemed to have gone up. Their utility bills were increasing, in spite of their conservation efforts. They wished they could do more traveling, but they doubted they could afford it. They were beginning to feel they should cut down on their bowling and golf in order to save money. They wondered if they were being imprudent in not saving more for their old age. They had not been living on a budget, so they decided their first effort should be to prepare a budget.

Dick and Jane's Budget

Dick and Jane kept track of their expenditures for two months, reviewed their past year's cancelled checks and credit card expenditures, and prepared the following budget, which includes the cost for the additional travel they desired. Their personal expense budget is on the following page.

WS-I.4.1
Page 1

PERSONAL EXPENSE BUDGET

Prepared for:
DICK AND JANE
Date: JAN. 6, 1983

HOUSING

Mortgage Pmt. or Rent	$ none
Taxes and Insurance	1,500
Upkeep	500
Utilities	1,200
TOTAL HOUSING EXP.	$ 3,200

FOOD

Groceries & Misc.	$ 2,500
Dining Out	500
TOTAL FOOD	$ 3,000

CLOTHING

New Clothes	$ 900
Cleaning	100
TOTAL CLOTHING	$ 1,000

TRANSPORTATION

Car Payments & Ins.	$ 500
Gas, Oil & Maint	1,500
Other Trans.	none
TOTAL TRANS.	$ 2,000

RECREATION

Vacation & Travel	$ 5,000
Other Recreation	3,000
TOTAL RECREATION	$ 8,000 #

LIFE INSURANCE	$ none
MED & MED INS	$ 1,200
GIFTS & CHARITIES	$ 3,000 #
OTHER EXPENSES	$ 2,000

TOTAL BUDGETED EXPENSES	$ 23,400
INFLATION-IMPACTED EXPENSES	$ 12,400
INFLATION-FREE EXPENSES	$ 11,000 #

Next they computed the income tax on their pension and Social Security benefits. Since their income (including the tax-free income on their municipal bonds) did not exceed $32,000, they did not owe income tax on their Social Security benefits. They computed the tax due on their pension benefits to be $275.

They were now ready to make the assumptions needed to complete their financial plan. After some deliberation they came up with the following assumptions.

Inflation rate:	6%
Aft.-tax Earn on Inv.	7%
Social Sec. Index Fctr.	4%
Longevity (both)	20 yrs.

They prepared the following work sheet:

Your Plan — Retirees 53

WS-I.4.2
Page 1

FINANCIAL PLAN FOR RETIREMENT

Name __Dick and Jane__ Date __1-6-83__

Line	RETIREMENT BUDGET		Base Year
1.	INCOME		
2.	Pension		$ 10,000
3.	Soc. Sec.		9,000
4.	Total Income	L2 + L3	19,000
5.	EXPENSE		
6.	Inflation Free		11,000
7.	Inc. Tx. (Pens. & Soc. Sec.)		275
8.	Inflation-Impacted		12,400
9.	Total Expense	L6 + L7 + L8	23,675
10.	DEFICIT OR SURPLUS	L4 - L9	$ (4,675)

	INVESTMENT REQUIRED		Factor(1)	
11.	To Cover First-Year Deficit	L10/factor	.095	$ 49,211
12.	To Cover Incr. Infl.-Impacted Exp.			
13.	Impacted Expense Only	L8 x factor	7.84	97,216
14.	If Aft-Tx Earn is not = Infl.	L13 x factor	.89	86,522
15.	Soc. Sec. Contribution	L3 x factor	5.87	52,830
16.	Net Required	L14 - L15		33,692
17.	First-Year Surplus Contribution	L10/factor		(none)
18.	TOTAL INVESTMENT REQUIRED	L16 + L11 or L16 - L17		82,903

	YOUR PLAN			
19.	Existing Investments			$ 110,000
20.	Investments Required	L18		82,903
21.	Excess (Shortage) of Investments	L20 - L18		27,017
22.	Invest. By End of Planning Period	L21/factor	3.94	$ 106,447

(1) See Page 2 For Factors

	ASSUMPTIONS		
23.	Years of Retirement	20	yrs.
24.	Inflation Expectations	6	%
25.	% Annual Incr. in Soc. Sec.	4	%
26.	After-Tax Earnings on Invest. After Retirement	7	%

(c) Copyright 1986 by Robert W. Shaffer

They transferred the factors they had obtained to the following work sheet as shown below:

WS-I.4.2
Page 2

INSTRUCTIONS FOR COMPLETING WS-I.4.2

STEP 1. Obtain the dollar amounts to be shown on Lines 2, 3, 6, 7, 8 from previously completed work sheets. List your assumptions on Lines 23 through 27.

STEP 2. Use your assumptions to fill in the blanks under the column labeled COORDINATES on the supplemental work sheet below. Find the value of the factors by using the coordinates and the table in Exhibit 1 found at the end of Chapter 3, Section 1. Show the factor on the proper line on WS-I.3.3, Page 1.

SUPPLEMENTAL WORK SHEET

	COORDINATES		TABLE	FACTOR	SHOW ON LINE OF WS-I.4.2, PAGE 1
% Aft-Tx Earn Aft Retir.		Yrs. of Ret.			
7 %		20 Yrs.	A	.095	11 (If 1st Yr Deficit)
					17 (If 1st Yr Surplus)
% Inflation		Yrs. of Ret.			
6 %		20 Yrs.	D-1	7.84	13
% S.S. Incr.		Yrs. of Ret.			
4 %		20 Yrs.	D-1	5.87	15

AFT-TX EARN AFT RET (7 %) minus INFL ASSUMPTION (6 %) = 1 %
(DIFFERENCE)

IF DIFFERENCE IS ZERO
The Factor Is				1.0	14

IF DIFFERENCE MORE THAN ZERO
More By:		Yrs. of Ret.			
1 %		20 Yrs.	D-2	.89	14

IF THE DIFFERENCE IS LESS THAN ZERO
Less By:		Yrs. of Ret.			
xx %		xx Yrs.	D-3	xxx	14

% Aft-Tx Earn After Ret.		Yrs. of Retirement			
7 %		20 Yrs.	B	3.94	22

STEP 3. Complete the mathematical calculations called for in the instructions on WS-I.4.2, Page 1.

Review of Their Budget

Dick and Jane carefully reviewed their assumptions and mathematical calculations. They analyzed their plan. They were surprised but pleased to note that their investment portfolio would be essentially the same at the end of the planning period as it was at the beginning. They realized that they had not included the costs of replacing various major items, such as their automobile, television, and appliances, during their retirement. But they should have ample capital for those purposes. Their desire and ability for travel and recreation would decrease in later years, so annual expenses would probably not continue at the present level. Their home was debt free; and if they found the need for additional funds in the final years of their plan, they could always sell their home and use those funds to cover living expenses.

Over the next two weeks Dick spent some time analyzing how various alternative assumptions would alter their plan. The following is a summary of some of his findings:

Using 6% inflation, 7% after-tax earnings, and 4% Social Security indexing assumptions, he found their existing investments would sustain their life style for 30 years.

Using 8% inflation, 7% after-tax earnings, and 4% Social Security indexing assumptions, he found their existing investments would sustain their life style for 18 years.

Using 10% inflation, 7% after-tax earnings, and 4% Social Security indexing assumptions, he found their existing investments would sustain their life style for 13 years.

Using 12% inflation, 12% after-tax earnings, and 12% Social Security indexing assumptions, he found their existing investments would sustain their life style for 33 years.

Using 6% inflation, 7% after-tax earnings, and no Social Security indexing assumptions, he found their existing investments would sustain their life style for 17 years.

Learning from Their Plan

In reviewing the above, Dick reached two primary conclusions:

1. **THE FAILURE TO OBTAIN AN AFTER-TAX EARNINGS EQUAL TO, OR GREATER THAN, INFLATION CAN HAVE A DEVASTATING IMPACT ON THE INVESTMENTS REQUIRED TO SUSTAIN A LIFE STYLE.** Refer to Table D-2 and Table D-3 (Exhibit 1, Page 2 of Chapter 3) and note that with a 2% after-tax earnings greater than inflation,

over a 20-year period, one needs only 79% of the amount needed if after-tax earnings equals inflation. Conversely with an after-tax earnings 2% less than inflation, one needs 128% more, over a 20-year period, than the amount needed if after-tax earnings equals inflation.

2. **THE FUTURE POLICY OF THE U.S. GOVERNMENT, IN REGARD TO THE CONTINUED INDEXING OF SOCIAL SECURITY BENEFITS, IS OF GREAT IMPORTANCE TO RETIREES.** Refer to Table D-1 (Exhibit 1, Page 2 of Chapter 3). Note that with the 4% indexing policy assumed by Dick and Jane, their Social Security Benefit Contribution amounted to $52,830 [$9,000 x 5.87 = $52,830]. A 6% indexing, an amount equal to Dick's assumed inflation rate, would have offset $70,560 [$9,000 x 7.84 = $70,560].

The more he thought about his investments, the more Dick began to realize that perhaps he needed to reconsider whether he had actually made prudent investments. He had a minimal income tax liability, so were tax-free investments right for them? But of more importance, if the inflation rate increased, the return on their investments would not increase in proportion to the increase in inflation. In fact the value of their investments would decline.

At present they were receiving income of $7,700 on their bonds [$110,000 x .07 = $7,700]. If inflation increased by 2% to 8%, it was probable that investors would want at least a 9% return on bonds of the quality they held. Thus it could be predicted that the bonds would be worth only $85,556 [$7,700 divided by .09 = $85,556]. Dick resolved to talk to his banker and friends knowledgeable about investment alternatives and see if he could come up with investments more suited to their needs.

We can reach several conclusions as a result of having shared Dick and Jane's financial planning. They have ample investments to allow them to live the life style they desire in their retirement. The assumptions they used appear to be conservative. They retired five years ago so are probably around 70. Twenty years of longevity is possible if both are in good health. Inflation of 6% is reasonable, and they have resources to withstand even a 12% inflation if they are able to keep the earning power of their investments at or above the inflation rate. Their assumption that future policy may result in a Social Security indexing at less than the inflation rate is also conservative.

However, they need to become more involved in formulating an investment policy that will meet their needs and give them the flexibility to meet future economic possibilities. A static investment policy used in a changing and volatile economic climate often results in disaster.

PREPARING YOUR FINANCIAL PLAN

Retirees now have sufficient information to enable them to prepare a financial plan. The work sheets you will use are found in the appendix. First complete WS-1.4.1 (Personal Expense budget). Next review the work sheets that are associated with Chapters 1 and 2 of this section. WS-1.4.2 can be prepared by using this information and the appropriate factors found in Exhibit 1 of Chapter 3.

You should have no trouble completing WS-1.4.2 if you carefully follow the instructions. As you are preparing your plan you may find it helpful to review Dick and Jane's work sheet.

The next chapter in this section, Investment Alternatives and Strategies, will give you some thoughts on how to tailor an investment portfolio to best fit your individual needs.

Chapter 5

Investment Alternatives and Strategies

Investment Alternatives and Strategies

PART 1: INTRODUCTION

The Fable of Bill the Baker

This is a fable about Bill the Baker from Camelot. Camelot's National Motto is work hard, save, and make prudent investments. One of the Founding Fathers is remembered for having said: "A penny saved is a penny earned." Some years ago the government of Camelot went off the gold standard. Their currency could no longer be exchanged for gold. They searched for a substitute and decided on bread. "After all, bread is the staff of life," the Economics Minister pointed out. "Yes, and our youth use the term bread instead of money in their street language," the Minister of Education concurred. So, bread was substituted for gold as the backing for their unit of currency, which was the dollar. They started with one dollar convertible to one loaf of bread.

Bill's business was baking bread. He worked hard and baked a lot of bread. "I have lived up to the first part of our national motto," he decided. "Now I must save." So he saved 1000 loaves of bread. Not understanding the term PRUDENT INVESTOR, he went to the citizen who was in the business of warehousing bread and lending it to those who wanted to borrow bread. They called him a banker.

"A prudent investor is one who exchanges his bread for dollars and rents his dollars to the government," the banker advised Bill. "In this way your dollars will grow," he further explained. Bill was pleased because now he understood the meaning of the term PRUDENT INVESTOR. He arranged for his banker to take his 1000 loaves of bread, convert them into $1,000, and loan the dollars to the government.

Bill went back to baking bread and continued to work hard. At the end of the first year, the government sent him an interest check for $60. He remembered his father's telling him that money makes money. He was learning all the time. In a few days he received a bill from the government for $16.80. He did not understand, so he went to the banker. "The government charges you for the interest you earned from renting them money," his friendly banker advised. "You are one of the better workers: you make more bread, you save, and are a prudent investor; therefore you are in the 28 percent tax bracket."

Somehow that didn't seem quite right to Bill. But he was only a hard working baker; and if his banker, who had an MBA, said it was OK, he decided he should not question Camelot's economic system. He took the remaining $43.20 and told his banker to loan that to the government also.

Bill continued his rental program for ten years. Each year he was pleased to see that the income dollars he received from the government were greater, but he was somewhat disturbed that the government's bill for taxes also increased. Each year he had his banker reinvest what he had left over from his past year's rental income.

At the end of ten years, Bill's oldest son was ready for college. He was an excellent student, and Bill wanted him to be a banker. Bankers didn't seem to work as hard as he himself did. They made their living by explaining to others the meaning of PRUDENT INVESTMENTS. The best college was Liberal University. Most of the leaders of the government of Camelot were graduates of this prestigious institution. However, Liberal U. insisted that their tuition of 1200 loaves of bread be paid in advance.

Bill went to the bank and asked how many dollars he had in his account. The banker punched several keys on the computer terminal on his desk and the answer appeared: $1,526.43. Bill was pleased that he was a PRUDENT INVESTOR. He would have enough for Liberal U.'s tuition and something left over. Bill asked the banker to give him 1200 loaves of bread from his account. Instead the banker punched a few more keys on the computer terminal and replied, "You have only 787 loaves of bread in your account."

Bill was certain there was a mistake. He didn't quite trust computers. "I gave you 1,000 loaves of bread ten years ago, which we converted to $1,000, and we lent that to the government. They paid me interest for ten years. Surely I must be entitled to more than 1000 loaves of bread," he pointed out confidently.

An irritated look appeared on the banker's face as he replied: "Bill, where have you been? Surely you know we have averaged an eight percent inflation over the past ten years, and the dollar has lost a great deal of its value in relation to bread."

Bill felt his world collapsing. What had happened to his PRUDENT INVESTMENT?

He did remember that from time to time he had heard the subject of inflation mentioned, but he had been so busy baking bread that he hadn't taken the time to try to understand just what it meant.

That is the end of our fable. And, like all fables, there is a moral. The moral is, **DON'T!!!** Don't what? We will answer that question shortly.

Analysis

Let's analyze Bill's PRUDENT INVESTMENT. First, Bill converted his 1,000 loaves of bread into $1,000 and loaned dollars to the government. Second, for ten years the government had the use of the money and paid Bill a 6% return from which the government took back 28% for taxes. Each year Bill reinvested what he had left of his earnings. The results are shown in the following table:

? BILL'S PRUDENT INVESTMENT ?

Year End	Dollars	6% Return On Investments	Dollars Reinvested	With 8% Infl. Rate Purchasing Power of The Dollar
0	$1000.00			
1	$1043.20	$60.00	$43.20	$959.74
2	$1088.27	$62.59	$45.07	$924.43
3	$1135.28	$65.30	$47.01	$893.72
4	$1184.32	$68.12	$49.04	$867.35
5	$1235.49	$71.06	$51.16	$845.03
6	$1288.86	$74.13	$53.37	$826.53
7	$1344.54	$77.33	$55.68	$811.63
8	$1402.62	$80.67	$58.08	$800.14
9	$1463.22	$84.16	$60.59	$791.87
10	$1526.43	$87.79	$63.21	$786.68

In order to purchase 1200 loaves of bread, Bill would need $2,592.

The following charts illustrate what inflation does to the costs of goods and services and to the value of the dollar:

COST OF A LOAF OF BREAD
(Average Rate of Inflation)

Years	2%	4%	6%	8%	10%	12%
0	1.00	1.00	1.00	1.00	1.00	1.00
5	1.10	1.21	1.34	1.47	1.61	1.76
10	1.22	1.48	1.79	2.16	2.59	3.11
15	1.36	1.80	2.40	3.17	4.18	5.47
20	1.49	2.19	3.21	4.66	6.73	9.65
25	1.64	2.67	4.29	6.85	10.83	17.00
30	1.81	3.24	5.74	10.06	17.45	29.96

VALUE OF A DOLLAR
(Average Rate of Inflation)

Years	2%	4%	6%	8%	10%	12%
0	1.00	1.00	1.00	1.00	1.00	1.00
5	.91	.83	.75	.68	.62	.57
10	.82	.68	.56	.46	.39	.32
15	.74	.56	.42	.32	.24	.18
20	.67	.46	.31	.21	.15	.10
25	.61	.37	.23	.15	.09	.06
30	.55	.31	.17	.10	.06	.03

With this background, you can understand the moral of our fable.
DON'T

- Ignore the effects of inflation when you make an investment
- Let others make your investment strategy
- Assume that an investment that returns you more dollars is a prudent investment
- Become too busy making money to understand inflation
- Become inflexible in your investment policies
- Fail to explore new investment opportunities
- Prevent inflation from working for you instead of against you
- Become a victim of inflation
- Forget the tax consequences of investment returns

The purpose of the balance of this chapter is to give you a broad knowledge of the many and varied investment opportunities and to give you a basic understanding of how best to build an investment portfolio that will provide for your future financial needs. *A financial investment is utilizing your surplus money in a manner to best increase its purchasing power.* It can be accomplished by capital appreciation, a return on invested capital, or both. Listed below are some of the typical investment alternatives that can be used to build an investment portfolio.

INVESTMENT TERMINOLOGY

Loans
Examples of investment alternatives under this category include
- Passbook savings, certificates of deposit, and interest-bearing checking accounts
- Bonds and debentures (federal, state, municipal, and corporate)
- Money market funds
- Mutual funds and trusts investing in bonds
- Life insurance other than term insurance

Purchasing an Interest in a Business
Examples of investment alternatives under this category include
- Starting your own business or profession
- Common and preferred stocks
- Mutual funds investing in stocks
- Purchasing or selling stock options
- Limited partnerships
- Oil and gas — exploration, development, or producing wells
- Real estate — commercial, residential, or agriculture
- Equipment leasing

Purchasing Tangible Assets
Examples of investment alternatives under this category include
- Precious metals — gold, silver, platinum
- Precious gems — diamonds, rubies, sapphires
- Collectibles — antiques, coins, stamps
- Land — commercial, residential, farming
- Commodities — corn, wheat, pork, coffee, cotton

As you consider these investment opportunities, ask yourself certain questions.
1. Will I increase the real value of my assets?
    a. From dividends or interest received from the borrower or company?
    b. From appreciation in the value of the investment?
2. What are the risks?
    a. Will the original investment dollars be returned?
    b. Will the dollars returned have an equivalent purchasing power?

3. If I achieve my investment objectives, what portion of my gain will I share with the government as a result of the taxes due on the capital appreciation and/or the earnings obtained?
4. Without undue risk, can my opportunities be enhanced by leverage capital?
5. How liquid is the investment? Can I make a timely conversion of the investments into dollars without a substantial loss?

In order to answer the above questions, you should understand *marginal tax rates* and *leverage*.

Marginal Tax Rate

If you are not familiar with your marginal tax rate I suggest you obtain a copy of the latest Federal Income Tax Instructions and turn to the table entitled "Tax Rate Schedules." Let's say your 1987 taxable income was $38,000. Referring to page 37 of the 1987 instructions you would find:

Over—	But not over—		of the amount over—
28,000	45,000	4,080 + 28%	28,000

Since your taxable income is over $28,000 and less than $45,000, your marginal tax rate is 28 percent. In other words, the IRS would want 28 percent of all taxable income over $28,000 up to $45,000.

Your state and municipality may also have income taxes. If so, you can determine your marginal tax rate for these taxing bodies. Since state and municipal income taxes are deductible from taxable income on your federal taxes, the combined marginal tax rate would be your federal marginal tax rate plus one-half your state and municipal marginal tax rate.

Leverage

To answer question 4, you must understand leverage. Leverage is the use of borrowed money to get a higher rate of return on your investment. This can be accomplished if the interest rate on the loan is lower than the rate of return on the investment. The following two examples illustrate this principle.

Example 1.

You purchase a rental property with the intent of receiving income from the rent and appreciation in the value of the property. The price of the unit is $100,000. You make a down payment of $20,000 and obtain a mortgage for $80,000. Sometime in the future you sell the property.

	ORIGINAL PRICE	SELLING PRICE	
TOTAL	$100,000	$120,000	$80,000
MORTGAGE	80,000	80,000	80,000
EQUITY	20,000	40,000	NONE

In one case, with a 20 percent *increase* in value, you doubled the value of your investment. In the second, with a 20 percent *decline* in value, you lost your investment. Leverage can be a blessing or a curse.

Example 2.

You wish to make an investment of $1,000. You borrow $800 from the bank, at 6 percent interest, and invest $200 of your savings. Your $1,000 investment earns 10 percent. What will be the return on your $200?

	28% Marginal Tax Rate	
Income	$100	$1,000 x 10%
Interest Expense	48	$800 x 6%
Profit Before Income Tax	52	$100 − $48
Income Tax at 28% Tax Rate	(14.56)	$52 x 28%
Profit After Tax	37.44	$52 − $14.56
Return On $200 Investment	18.7%	$37.44 / $200

This example demonstrates the increase in return that the prudent use of borrowed funds (leverage) provides, as well as the effect that the marginal tax rate has on the return.

PART 2: INVESTMENT ALTERNATIVES

You will recall that the three investment alternatives are loans, purchasing an interest in a business, and purchasing tangible assets. Each of these alternatives are discussed below, together with how each meets the test of the five questions.

LOANS

These investment opportunities return interest for the use of the money. The period of time you agree to loan your savings varies. For some investments of this type, you can redeem your funds at any time, while for others you commit your funds for several years. Long-term loans with a minimum risk usually return approximately three percent more than the anticipated long-term inflation rate. Higher risk investments usually bring higher investor return. Short-term borrowing rates tend to fluctuate more with the money supply and the demand for money. If the supply of money is short (more people want to borrow than want to loan), short-term money costs will increase. The Federal Reserve Board also influences the supply of money by various actions and thus has a considerable influence on the cost of short-term money. If you commit your money for a definite period but decide to liquidate before that period expires, you may suffer a loss of earnings. Your income will be taxed at your marginal tax rate. Leverage is not usually used with this type of investment.

Historically, investments of this type have been considered prudent investments because of your assurance that your invested dollars will be returned. However, in times of high inflation, this category of investments has suffered severe losses of purchasing power. In order for you to protect your purchasing power, your after-tax return should equal the inflation rate. In Bill the Baker's case, with an 8 percent inflation, he should have been receiving 12.5 percent before taxes since he was in the 28 percent marginal tax bracket. If he had been in a 15 percent marginal tax bracket, he could have maintained his purchasing power with a 10.39 percent before-tax return. The proof of this statement is shown below:

Return on Investment	12.5%	10.39%
Investment at Beginning of Year	$1000.00	$1,000.00
Earnings	125.00	103.90
28% Income Tax	35.00	
15% Income Tax		15.59
After-Tax Dollars	90.00	88.31
% After-Tax Earnings	9.00%	8.83%
Purchasing Pwr. Loss (1)	90.00	88.31
$ Purch Pwr. Reward	00.00	00.00

(1) Investment Dollar plus Earnings times 8% inflation

Interest-earning checking accounts, passbook savings, and money market funds are liquid since the amount of your investment can be withdrawn upon demand. Certificates of deposit require you to commit your funds for periods of time ranging from three months to four or more years. There are many other investment opportunities similar to certificates of deposits, such as treasury bills, banker's acceptance notes, and federal agency issues.

Corporations, governmental entities, and institutions frequently borrow money by issuing bonds or debentures. Bonds are secured by the assets of the issuing entity, while debentures are backed by the credit of the issuer. Organizations that evaluate the credit worthiness of the issuers of new bonds publish their ratings. These ratings fall into six categories. Many investors believe that a bond or debenture should receive an AAA, AA, or A rating if it is to be considered an investment-grade security. Anything with a lower rating would be considered a speculative investment. The higher the rating, the lower the return to the investor. The maturity dates of bonds or debenture varies, but 30 years is typical.

There are many different features of bonds that should be analyzed when making a decision as to whether a particular bond is a candidate for your investment portfolio. Some bonds have a convertible feature that provides that under certain conditions the bond can be converted to a certain number of shares of the common stock of the issuing company. Others provide that at some future date the company will have the option of redeeming the bond with the payment of some premium over the purchase price of the bond. Municipal bonds are tax free, that is, their interest is not subject to federal income taxes (and generally state taxes) in the state in which they are issued. If you are in a high tax bracket, the benefits are obvious. The rate of return on tax-free bonds is, of course, less than for bonds whose interest is taxable.

The resale value of a bond is affected by its return as compared to investments of similar risks and the length of time until the bond matures. Let us take the case of the bond purchased by Bill the Baker.

Historically, for the most prudent investments, the yield has been approximately three percent plus the anticipated inflation rate. Using this assumption we could conclude that the inflation expectation was three percent at the time Bill loaned Camelot his money. (Bill's six-percent return minus three-percent yield equals three percent.) You will recall the banker advised Bill that they had been experiencing an eight-percent inflation. This would suggest that, during the ten years that Camelot had Bill's money, any new investment in government bonds would have yielded 11 percent. If Bill had wished to sell his bond at any time during the ten-year period, a purchaser would have offered him an amount that would yield 11 percent. Since he received $60 in interest on his $1,000 investment each year, the investor would have offered him $545 [$60 divided by .11]. Many bond prices are quoted in financial papers, and if Bill had been a reader of the *Wall Street Journal* and followed the price being paid for his bond, he would have known what was happening to the purchasing power of his investment.

In a period of rising inflation and interest rates, the resale value of a bond declines. Conversely, the value will rise in a period of declining inflation and declining interest rates. The increase in value during declining money costs offers investors in bonds a chance to realize capital gains in addition to interest income.

Bond mutual funds and bond trusts allow you to purchase a share of a professionally selected and managed portfolio of bonds. You participate in the income and changing value of the portfolio in the same ratio your investment has to the total value of the fund. The management of the fund charges a small fee for over-seeing the fund. The evaluation and trading of bonds is complex. Unless you are knowledgeable, a fund or trust may be the best method for you to invest in bonds. Each fund has certain objectives and invests in certain types of bonds. For example, some purchase and trade only in municipal tax-free bonds.

During periods when interest rates are high and money is tight, borrowers will often pay very high rates of interest for large sums of money. Usually these high rates apply only to someone willing to loan $100,000 or more. Few of us have this amount of liquid assets. So, money market funds were conceived. The fund will pool your modest investment with many other modest investments to create a pool of funds that can benefit from the same investment opportunities previously given only large investors. The rate varies based on the short-term money supply. The funds are liquid, in that your dollars can be withdrawn on demand and you can often even write checks on your funds. During the most recent period of high interest costs, the prime rate was 20 percent, and you could receive as much as an 18 percent return from these funds.

Life insurance (other than term insurance) is a combination of an insurance policy and an investment. The insurance company, in effect, borrows from you the amount your premium exceeds their cost of insuring your life and invests the surplus. Usually the invested portion of the premium has given very modest returns, compared to what you could obtain from other types of investments.

PURCHASING AN INTEREST IN A BUSINESS
Common Stock

The most typical method of purchasing an interest in a business is to buy shares in a publicly-traded company. Their shares are bought and sold on the New York, American, Over the Counter, or a regional exchange. Your participation in the financial health of the company is at the same ratio that the value of your investment is to the total value of all the equity owners.

If the company earns enough to pay all its expenses and has some left over, it makes a profit; and usually you will receive a share of the profit. The management of the company may declare a dividend, or they may decide to reinvest all of the profits back into the business. Most companies do a combination of both. The ratio of stock price to earnings is called the price-earnings (PE) ratio. The percentage of the profits they pay out in dividends is the payout ratio.

The dividend payment is taxable to you at your marginal tax rate. If the company reinvests your profit back into the company, it should result in the growth of the business, and the value of your stock should appreciate. If you sell your shares for more than you paid for them, the increase is called a capital gain.

The assurance that you will receive your dollars back is less than if you lend your money, but your chances of being able to maintain your purchasing power may improve.

If you purchase stocks in a publicly-traded company, you can sell the stock through a broker and receive your money in five working days.

Preferred Stock

Preferred-stock holders are also owners of the business. However, their rights differ from those of the common-stock holder. If a profit is made, they have first rights to the profit. The return is stipulated, and thus the owners are limited in the amount of return they receive. Some preferred stocks have cumulative dividend provision, which means that if for some period the company doesn't make a sufficient profit to pay the preferred-stock dividend, the holders will receive back payment of dividends before any return can be paid to the common-stock holder. Some preferred stocks have a conversion feature, which means that the preferred shares can be exchanged for a specified number of common shares.

The value of the share of preferred stock is influenced more by the rate of the dividend (as compared to current returns available from other investment opportunities) than by the profitability of the company. Thus their value tends to decrease with an increase in interest rates, and vice versa.

Limited Partnership

There are many different types of limited partnerships. In each there is a general partner and many limited partners. The general partner organizes the venture and either manages the enterprise or arranges to hire managers. Most of the capital is advanced by the limited partners, and the rewards of the venture are shared by both the general and limited partners.

The limited partner thus retains professional management and is relieved of record keeping. Usually this type of investment has very limited liquidity. The dollar risks, as compared to our previously discussed investment alternatives, is high. However, the risk is usually limited to the amount the limited partner has invested in the partnership.

There are many types of businesses that have limited partner opportunities. The most prevalent are oil and gas, real estate, and equipment leasing. Limited partnerships have some very attractive tax benefits for those in the higher tax brackets. For example, the use of leverage, the possibility of receiving capital gains, the availability of depreciation, investment tax credits, and depletion allowances allow for tax deductions and tax shelters.

It is my observation that many more individuals have lost money investing in limited partnerships than have made money. All too often the desire to obtain income tax write-offs dulls the investor's perception of the risks inherent in the venture. Some of the general partners have proved to be incompetent and/or unscrupulous. Individuals should consider making this type of investment only if they are well informed or only with the advice of their attorney or tax accountant.

PURCHASE OF TANGIBLE ASSETS

None of the investments in this category provide interest or dividend income. The hope of the investor is that the value of the purchased asset will increase. This will occur if the demand for the asset exceeds the supply. In most cases the sales commission is sizeable, and considerable appreciation must occur before you will make money on the resale of the asset.

You have no assurance that your original dollars will be returned or that purchasing power will be maintained. Liquidity for the most part is poor. Leverage can be used in purchasing land and commodities.

CONCLUSIONS

Only the most common and popular investment alternatives have been discussed. Many others are available. Before considering investing in most alternatives, each individual should be assured he or she is adequately informed as to the risks and potential rewards. A systematic approach to the acquisition of investment knowledge is covered later in this chapter.

PART 3: INVESTMENT STRATEGY

The task of an investor is to select one or more investment alternatives in which to invest your dollars. The strategy is to *minimize risk* and *maximize reward*. The risk you are concerned with is the loss of part or all of invested dollars. The reward sought is an appreciation in the value and/or return on the investment to increase purchasing power. In general we can say:

- No-risk investments will always provide low or negative purchasing power rewards.
- Low-risk investments will usually provide low purchasing power rewards.
- Medium-risk investments will frequently provide a medium level of purchasing power rewards.
- High-risk investments will occasionally provide high levels of purchasing power rewards.

A skillful investor will always be attempting to reduce the risk or increase the probability and level of the reward.

ATTRIBUTES OF THE SKILLED INVESTOR

To be a good investor, you should possess and use your knowledge, imagination, decisiveness, and savings.

Knowledge

Investing requires a broad general knowledge about various forces that impact or influence the economic well being of the candidates selected as investment possibilities. You need an understanding of the causes and effects of inflation, tax policies and provisions, the forces behind recessions and recoveries, the changing needs and wants of society, the interdependence of world markets, political philosophies, economic theories, world affairs, and much more.

You probably spent much of your schooling and training preparing to earn a living. You learned how to make money, but not how to invest it. Even those individuals whose vocation calls for them to deal with money or economics often have highly developed specialized knowledge but lack the broad knowledge required to be successful investors.

Fortunately, the required knowledge is not difficult to acquire and is readily available. Your newspaper, television programs, periodicals, seminars, and business journals are but a few of many sources for the information you will need. You should develop the habit of spending a part of your time obtaining information useful in making investment choices.

You also learn by doing. You will make mistakes; everyone does. Analyze why, and use the failure as an opportunity to learn.

Imagination

You may have the mistaken idea that only those with great intelligence can be successful investors. If this were so, there would be a high correlation between high intelligence and great wealth. There is not. Rather, what is needed is imagination, the ability to think independently and to anticipate change.

When asked for the secret of his success, one noted and successful investor answered, "Buy low, sell high." Stock brokers have a saying, "Buy on gloom, sell on glory." In other words, when everyone thinks the bottom is about to drop out of the market, buy. When they think it is going through the roof, sell. When everyone wants to sell, you can get a bargain. When many want to buy what you have for sale, you can get top dollar.

When we have double-digit inflation, it takes imagination to foresee declining inflation rates. When we are in a serious recession, it takes imagination to foresee an upturn in the economy. In periods of oil shortages, it is difficult to perceive the coming of oil gluts.

Be an independent thinker. Listen to all the analysts, advisors, economists, and politicians you can. Read all the financial newspapers, market letters, and presidential messages on annual reports that you can find. But don't blindly believe any of them. Listen to their logic, not the smoothness of their words or rhetoric. Explore alternative scenarios and make up your own mind. You don't have to be right all the time. Just being right more often than the average can make you a successful investor.

Decisiveness

Some individuals have the knowledge and the imagination to pick good investments, but they don't have the courage to make a decision. They watch the stock they picked to be a winner go from $40 a share to $70 and never have the courage to step in and take a position in the market. Others will purchase a stock and not have the courage to admit they made a mistake. Successful investors are not afraid to admit a mistake and take their losses. They use their mistakes as an opportunity to learn. In this way they are constantly improving their investing skill and thus are able to reduce risks and increase rewards.

The Discipline To Save

The requirement to have savings to invest is so obvious you are probably wondering why I bother to include it. I have heard many people say, "My expenses are so high I just can't save." And yet they may well have two new cars in the garage, a boat in the back yard, and a second home at the sea shore. The problem isn't that they haven't sufficient income to save. The problem is that they put saving low on the priority of what they want to do with their money. To have money to invest, you must put savings high on the priority list of how you are going to use your money. The earlier in life you establish a systematic savings plan, the easier it will be for you to acquire sufficient assets to provide you with a full and happy retirement. For example: If you start at 25 years of age putting $2,000 a year in an IRA account which earns 10 percent, by the time you are 65 your account will be worth $885,185.

Knowledge, imagination, and decisiveness can be likened to the generic program that exists in the central processing unit of a computer. It lies dormant and useless until the input of information allows it to begin processing data. Therefore, the next step in strategic investing is to determine what input is required. Consideration of the facts and assumptions listed below is suggested.

IMPACT OF AGE

In your early years you will probably have limited savings. High-risk investments are generally considered imprudent. Therefore, low-risk investments are the suggested use of investment funds during this period of your life.

Likewise, as you approach retirement, it is prudent to again avoid high-risk investments. It would be tragic to have saved and invested all of your working career and find your investment portfolio decimated by high-risk investments.

ASSUMED INFLATION RATE

Your assumption as to future inflation rates should have a major influence on your investment strategy. The higher your marginal tax rate, the more imperative this becomes. Throughout most of our history, successful investors were usually not overly concerned with inflation. The high rates of inflation we had during the last of the 70s, however, created a need for changes in investment strategies. If you believe that the average inflation rate will be more than four percent, your investment strategy should be oriented to protecting purchasing power. Remember Bill the Baker. If you assume a low rate of inflation, you may want to take less risk with your investment dollar.

MARGINAL TAX RATE

The higher your marginal tax bracket, the more Uncle Sam will share in your investment rewards. Inflation and high marginal tax rates make the attainment of purchasing power rewards difficult. Medium- and high-risk investments may be required to maintain purchasing power. To aid you in determining your required return to maintain purchasing power, WS-I.5.1 is provided. Please complete it at this time.

TAX CODE PROVISIONS

The tax code has provisions designed to encourage certain types of investments. (It might be considered cynical to suggest there may also be other reasons.) Regardless, the result is that Uncle Sam becomes your partner in sharing the risks for these investment alternatives. Tax code provisions dealing with tax write-offs and tax deferrals are very complex. The average individual does not have the time to comprehend them fully. If you decide to select investments in this category, you should develop a general understanding of their provisions and seek the advice of a professional (such as an accountant or attorney specializing in tax matters) before making such an investment.

LEVERAGE

We have previously discussed leverage and how it can be applied to increase purchasing power rewards. If used judiciously, it can be an important tool in increasing the rewards for certain types of investment.

DIVERSIFICATION

No one bats 100 percent in their investment selections. If you have limited funds for investment, you must recognize this fact in your investment strategy. If you can purchase only a few shares of common stock in one company, your chance of success is limited. If you can invest in only one oil and gas exploration through a limited partnership, your chance of hitting it big is doubtful. With limited investment funds you will probably wish to be concerned with the dollar risk and consider diversification by using mutual funds, or some similar investment alternative, until you can build sufficient investment funds to allow you investment diversification.

INVESTMENTS STRATEGY OUTLINE

The summary that follows outlines the suggested investment strategy discussed to this point.

Investment Strategy

The Process Of Investing Involves
   Selecting Investment Alternatives Such As
      Loaning Money To Others
      Purchasing A Portion Of A Business
      Purchasing Tangibles
   And Using Your
      Knowledge
      Imagination
      Decisiveness
      Savings
   And Considering Your
      Age
      Assumed Inflation Rate
      Marginal Tax Rate
      Tax Code Provisions
      Leverage
      Diversification
   You Make Investment Choices To
      Maximize Purchasing Power Rewards And
      Minimize The Risks Of Losing Investment Dollars

"Coin Flip" Investment Scenario

The following tale illustrates some of the investment strategy principles:

A friend suggests an investment opportunity. You are to flip a coin, and if it comes up heads, you win. As a reward you will, of course, keep the coin; and he will give you $1.25. If you lose, he gets your coin.

You analyze the risks and rewards. You know you have a 50 percent chance of throwing a head and receiving a 125 percent reward. And, conversely, you have a 50 percent chance of throwing a tail and losing your investment. You make the following investment analysis:

Investment Alternatives and Strategies

Number of Investments		Invested	Reward	Return Per Invest.	Total Return
5	Heads	$1.00	$1.25	$2.25	$11.25
5	Tails	$1.00	($1.00)	none	none
	Total				$11.25
	Less Original Investment				$10.00
	Profit				$ 1.25
	Percent Profit [$1.25/$10]				12.5%

A stately looking gentleman you know as Uncle Sam informs you that since he is providing for your security, general welfare, etc., he is going to take 28 percent of your profits (your marginal tax rate). So, you continue your calculations as follows:

Number of Investments		Invested	Reward	Return Per Invest.	Total Return
5	Heads	$1.00	$1.25	$2.25	$11.25
5	Tails	$1.00	($1.00)	none	none
	Total				$11.25
	Less Original Investment				$10.00
	Profit				$ 1.25
	Percent Profit				12.5%

Tax @ 28%	.35
After-Tax Profit	.90
Percent After-Tax Profit	9.0%

But Uncle Sam continues. In order to stimulate the economy, he is going to increase the money supply, and the result will be an inflation rate of 8 percent. So back to more calculations as follows:

Number of Investments		Invested	Reward	Return Per Invest.	Total Return
5	Heads	$1.00	$1.25	$2.25	$11.25
5	Tails	$1.00	($1.00)	none	none
	Total				$11.25
	Less Original Investment				$10.00
	Profit				$ 1.25
	Percent Profit				12.5%

Tax @ 28%	.35
After-Tax Profit	.90
Percent After-Tax Profit	9.0%

Infl. Tax of 8% ($11.25 x .08)	$0.90
Purchasing Power Reward	$0.00

You look at your analysis and determine that inflation will erode the value of the $11.25 you received for tossing five heads by 8 percent, or $0.90. Since your after-tax reward is only $.90, the net result is that you will only maintain your purchasing power.

You determine that through the acquisition of knowledge and skills you can improve your investment odds to a 60 percent success ratio. That is, you will be able to average six heads and four tails on the toss of ten coins. Using this risk-reward ratio you again make an analysis as follows:

Number of Investments		Invested	Reward	Return Per Invest.	Total Return
6	Heads	$1.00	$1.25	$2.25	$13.50
4	Tails	$1.00	($1.00)	none	none
	Totals				$13.50
	Original Investment				$10.00
	Profit				$ 3.50
	Income Tax @ 28%				$ .98
	After-Tax Profit				$ 2.52
	Infl. Penalty of 8% [13.50 x .08]				$ 1.08
	Purchasing Power Increase				$ 1.44
	% Purchasing Power Return On $10 Inv.				14.4%

Even though the "coin flip" investment scenario is not entirely analogous to actual investment situations, it can be used to illustrate several investment principles.

Investments are gambles. Your chances of success improve if you understand the odds and analyze your risk-reward ratios. In times of inflation, not to invest is a gamble. Note that if you elected not to participate in your friend's "coin flip" investment program and buried the $10 in a can in the back yard, with 10 percent inflation you would lose $1.00 of purchasing power the first year.

Diversification minimizes the risk of investing. If you were to invest your entire $10 on one toss of the coin, you would stand a 50 percent chance of losing your entire investment.

Because of income taxes, Uncle Sam receives a portion of your investment reward. The impact of income taxes should be considered in evaluating investment alternatives.

The goal of any investment strategy should be at least the maintenance of, and hopefully the reward of, an increase in purchasing power.

You can reduce the risks associated with specific investment alternatives if you have the proper knowledge and imagination. The result is that your rewards will be greater than for someone without such knowledge.

If you postpone the pleasure of consumption, save money, and invest, you should receive a reward. The expected reward is an increase in purchasing power of your investment. Whether, in fact, you do receive your reward depends upon your skills in investing. The skillful investor will attempt to minimize dollar risk and maximize purchasing power reward. During periods of inflation it is difficult to make investments offering both low-dollar risks and medium purchasing power rewards. The difficulty increases as your marginal tax rate increases.

The dollar risk for individuals investing in a certificate of deposit would be none, for they would be assured of retaining their invested dollars. However, whether they would receive a purchasing power reward would depend upon the before-tax return they received on the investment and their marginal tax rate.

For most of the investment alternatives, the dollar risk and purchasing power rewards depend upon a number of unknown future developments. Since no one can predict the future with absolute certainty, the inclination to avoid investment risks is understandable. However, the failure to invest savings ensures a serious erosion of purchasing power, even with a modest inflation rate. For example: With an average annual inflation rate of 6 percent, your dollar will lose 25 percent of its purchasing power in five years. So, invest you must if you hope to have investment income for the financial needs of retirement.

Using your knowledge and imagination, you should consider various investment alternatives. Then evaluate, to the best of your ability, the dollar risks and purchasing power rewards, before making your decisions as to how you should invest your savings.

RISK-REWARD GRID

The RISK-REWARD GRID is provided as a tool to assist you in arriving at your decision.

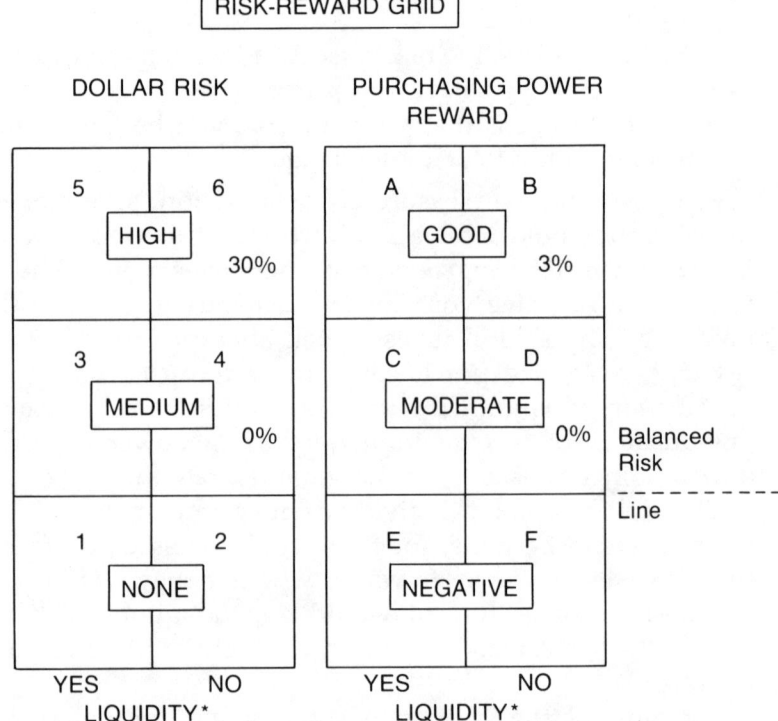

Balanced Risk Line — After-tax earnings required to protect purchasing power.

*Liquidity — The ability to redeem an asset at any time without the loss of principal and/or earnings.

The following thoughts and observations will assist you in understanding the purpose for, and facilitate the use of, the RISK-REWARD GRID in making investment decisions.

Liquidity

To be considered liquid, an investment should be readily convertible to dollars without a potential loss of dollar and/or stated returns. An investment in money market funds would be considered liquid. A one-year certificate of deposit would not, since early withdrawal could result in a reduction in earned interest. Stocks and bonds would not be considered liquid because, if the per-share price of the stock, or face value of the bond, were lower than your invested price, their sale would result in a loss of investment dollars. (Note: The definition of liquidity used here will differ from many you may find.) There are two primary reasons why you should keep a portion of your investment portfolio liquid.

Emergencies

If an emergency arises that requires you to convert a portion of your investments into cash, it is preferable that you lose neither dollars, nor return on the redeemed asset. It is suggested that you keep liquid an amount equal to three month's take-home pay to be used as an emergency fund.

Investment Flexibility

From time to time you may wish to have a pool of liquid assets available to take advantage of perceived investment opportunities. For example, you may believe a bear market (stocks are declining) is about to end, and a bull market (stocks are increasing in price) is about to commence. You may wish to accumulate liquid assets to make investment purchases at some future date. The amount of liquidity you wish to maintain for this purpose is dependant upon conditions and your preferences.

Dollar Risk

It is easy to identify no-dollar risks. Medium- or high-dollar risks are more difficult to quantify. If your investment choice is a blue chip stock whose present price-earnings ratio is near an all time low, the prospect for the loss of investment dollars should probably be considered medium. An investment in an exploratory oil and gas limited partnership should be classified a high-dollar-risk investment.

I have suggested a zero to thirty percent bracket as the parameters of a medium-dollar-risk investment. If you elect to use the grid as an investment tool, you may wish to establish other parameters.

Purchasing Power Reward

In order to achieve a purchasing power reward, the after-tax return on your investment must exceed the inflation rate. This level of return is identified on the RISK-REWARD GRID as the Balance Risk Line. For a few investments (such as money market funds) the only variable that must be assumed is the inflation rate. You should know your marginal tax rate. For example, if you are in the 28 percent marginal tax bracket, you will require a 8.33 percent before-tax return to obtain a 6 percent after-tax rate. A purchasing power reward will require a higher return.

The loss of a portion of your investment dollars is also a loss of purchasing power, unless we are in a period of disinflation.

The increase in the value of a marketable asset is an increase of purchasing power. Therefore, in estimating purchasing power reward you should consider a possible change in asset value, as well as the return on the investment. I have established arbitrary standards of zero to three percent for a moderate purchasing power reward. You may elect to set other parameters.

The following is an example of how you might go about making an analysis of an investment to determine purchasing power reward.

You are interested in a stock currently selling for $30 per share. It pays a dividend of $3. You anticipate the value of the stock will increase to $40 in a year. You further assume that we will experience a 6 percent inflation rate over the next year. You are in the 28 percent tax bracket.

You make the following analysis:

Capital Gain (before tax)	$10.00	($40−$30=$10)
Income Tax on Capital Gain	$ 2.80	($10x.28=$2.80)
After-Tax Income	$ 7.20	($10−$2.80=$7.20)
Dividend Income	$ 3.00	
Income Tax on Dividend	$ 0.84	($3x.28=$.84)
After-Tax Dividend Income	$ 2.16	($3−$.84=$2.16)
Total After-Tax Gain	$ 9.36	($7.20+$2.16)

Investment	$30.00	
After-Tax Return	31.2 %	($9.36/$30)
Purch. Pwr. Value Decline @ 6% Infl.	$ 2.36	($30.00+$9.36)x.06
Purchasing Power Reward	$ 7.00	($9.36−$2.36)
% PURCHASING POWER REWARD	23.3 %	($7.00/$30.00)

You would classify this investment opportunity as a *good purchasing power reward*. If you feel reasonably confident that the value of the shares will not decrease, you would probably classify the dollar risk as *medium*.

Every investment should receive a dollar-risk and a purchasing power reward rating, as well as a determination of the liquidity of the assets.

The ideal investment alternative is a 1-A investment — a liquid no-dollar risk with a good purchasing power reward. Such investments probably do not exist. The investment to be avoided is a 6-F investment — a high-dollar risk with a negative purchasing power reward. Numerous conmen and promoters push these types of investments. A good adage for investors to remember is, "If it seems too good to be true, it probably is."

The backbone of most good investment portfolios are medium-dollar-risk investments (4) with moderate (D) or good (B) purchasing power rewards.

As your investment knowledge matures, and the possibility for diversification increases, you may wish to take some 6-B investments (high-dollar risks with good purchasing power rewards). Remember, in our "coin-flip" investment scenario we had a 50-percent dollar risk for each investment opportunity. However, by making several investments we reduced the dollar risk and had a possibility of receiving a purchasing power reward.

George's Investments

To understand the practical application of these investment principles, consider the hypothetical experience of George.

George inherits $20,000 which he decides to invest. He is in the 28 percent marginal tax bracket. George estimates a 6 percent average inflation rate over the next few years; and he predicts an improving business climate during the next year. He calculates his minimum-risk return for ordinary income to be 8.33 percent. He selects and analyzes four investment alternatives, (1) bonds, (2) common stocks, (3) real estate, (4) gold.

Bonds

AA Corporate Bonds—Yield 12.5%
Corporate Bond	$1000.00	
Dollar Yield	$125.00	($1,000x.125)
Tax @ 28%	$36.00	($125x.28)
After-Tax Yield	$89.00	($125−$36)
% Dollar Return	8.9 %	($89/$1000)
Purchasing Power Decline @ 6%	$65.34	($1000+$89x.06)
Purchasing Power Gain	$23.66	($89−$65.34)
% Purchasing Power Reward	2.37%	($23.66/$1000)

Municipal Tax-Free Bonds—Yield 9.0%
Municipal Bond	$1000.00	
Dollar Yield	$90.00	($1000x.09)
Tax (No Tax)	$0.00	
After-Tax Yield	$90.00	
% Dollar Return	9.00%	($90/$1000)
Purchasing Power Decline @ 6%	$65.40	($1000+$90x.06)
Purchasing Power Gain	$24.60	($90−$65.40)
% Purchasing Power Reward	2.46%	($24.60/$1000)

Stocks

George is familiar with the XYZ company and estimates they will have a 15 percent increase in earnings in the coming year. He further projects that they will increase their current dividend by 15 percent. Because of the improving business climate, he believes the market will rise and XYZ's price-earnings ratio will improve to 9. He therefore makes the following calculations:

XYZ Company

Existing Per Share Price	$32.00	
PE Ratio	8	
Current Yr. Earn.	$ 4.00	
Payout Ratio	20.00%	
Dividend	$ 0.80	
Incr. Earnings Next Year	15.00%	
Next Yrs. Earn.	$ 4.60	($4x115%)
New P.E. Ratio	9	
Next Yr. Stock Price	$41.40	($4.60x9)
Next Yr. Dividends	$ 0.92	($4.60x20%)

Capital Gain & Dividend	$10.32	($41.40 − $32.00) + $.92
Tax @ .28%	$ 2.89	($10.32x28%)
After-Tax Income	$ 7.43	($10.32 − $2.89)
After-Tax Return	23.22%	($7.43/$32)
Loss Purch. Power @ 6% Infl.	$ 2.54	($41.40 + $.92)x.06
Purch. Pwr. Reward	$ 4.89	($7.43 − $2.54)
Purch. Power Return	15.29%	($4.89/$32)

Real Estate — Residential

With the help of a real estate agent, George finds a rental unit he can purchase for $100,000. He consults his banker who tells him he can obtain an $80,000 mortgage at 12-percent interest. He further advises him the monthly mortgage payments will be $731.79. George decides he will plan to sell the unit in five years, so he asks the banker how much the mortgage will be after five years. The banker advises him that at the end of five years it will be paid down to $77,505. His next question to the banker is "How much will the unit be worth if it appreciates 6 percent a year for five years?" (George has assumed an average of 6-percent inflation over the five-year period and further that the increased value of real estate will track inflation.) The banker consults some tables and advises him that the value of the unit will appreciate to $133,823. George makes the following calculations.

	Beginning of 1st yr.	End of 5th yr.	
Value	$ 100,000	$133,823	
Mortgage	$ 80,000	$77,505	
Equity	$ 20,000	$56,318	
PROFIT & LOSS PROJECTION			
Income ($800 Per Month Rent)	$ 9,600	Estimate	
Expense			
Taxes, Ins. Etc.	$ 700		
Mortgage	$ 8,781	($731.79x12)	
Upkeep	$ 1,000	Estimate	
Deprec. (27.5 Yrs. Straight Line)	$ 3,636	($100,000/27.5)	
Total Expense	$ 14,117		
Operating Loss	$ −4,517	($9,600 − $14,117)	
Tax Savings @ 28% Marg. Tax Rate	$ −1,265	($4,517x.28)	
After-Tax Loss	$ −3,252	($4,517 − $1,265)	

	Beginning of 1st yr.	End of 5th yr.
ANNUAL CASH FLOW		
In		
Rent	$ 9,600	
Tax Savings	$ 1,265	
Total	$ 10,865	
Out		
Mortgage	$ 8,781	
Taxes, Ins., Etc.	$ 700	
Upkeep	$ 1,000	
After-Tax Loss	$ 3,252	
Total	$ 13,733	
Net Cash Flow	$ −2,868	($10,865−$13,733)
Capital Gain		
Selling Price	$ 133,823	
6% Selling Commission	$ 8,029	($133,823x.06)
Net	$ 125,794	($133,823−$8,029)
Purchase Price	$ 100,000	
Depreciation Taken Over 5 Yrs.	$ 18,180	($3,636x5)
Net	$ 81,820	($100,000−$18,180)
Taxable Gain	$ 43,974	($125,794−$81,820)
Tax @ .28%	$ 12,313	($43,974x.28)
Net After-Tax	$ 31,661	($43,974−$12,313)
5-Year Gain/Loss Analysis		
5-Year Cash Flow	$ −14,340	($2,868x5)
After-Tax Gain From Sale	$ 31,661	
Decrease in Mortgage	$ 2,495	($80,000−$77,505)
5-Year Dollar Gain/Loss	$ 19,816	(−14340+31661+2495)
Average Dollar Gain Per Year	$ 3,963	($19,816/5)
% Dollar Return	19.82%	($3.963/$20,000)
Purch. Power Value Decline with 6% Infl.		
Dollar Value of Gain	$ 19,816	
End of Year 1	$ 18,627	($19,816x.94)
End of Year 2	$ 17,509	($18,627x.94)
End of Year 3	$ 16,458	($17,509x.94)
End of Year 4	$ 15,471	($16,458x.94)
End of Year 5	$ 14,543	($15,471x.94)
Avg. Purchasing Power Gain Per Year	$ 2,909	($14,543/5)
Average Purchasing Power Return	14.55%	($2,909/$20,000)

Gold

A commodity broker assures George that gold will appreciate by 25 percent over the next year.

Present Price of Gold	$400	per troy ounce
Price Projected by End of Yr.	$500	($400x1.25)
Gain	$100	($500−$400)
Capital Gain Tax	$ 28	($100x.28)
After-Tax Gain	$ 72	(100−$28)
After-Tax Return	18%	($72/$400)
Loss Purch. Pwr. @ 6% Infl.	$ 30	(500x.06)
Purchasing Power Reward	$ 42	($72−$30)
% Purch. Pwr. Reward	10.5%	($42/$400)

George makes a risk-reward analysis as follows:

RISK-REWARD ANALYSIS

	After-Tax Return	Purch. Power Return	Dollar Risk	Purch. Power Reward
Bonds				
Municipal	9.00%	2.46%	4	D
AA Corporate	8.90%	2.37%	4	D
XYZ Company	23.22	15.29%	4	B
Real Estate	19.82%	14.55%	4	B
Gold	18.00%	10.50%	6	B

George studied the above analysis and eliminated the bonds as candidates for investment. While he liked the safety of the dollar risk, he concluded that the slight increase in purchasing power did not meet his investment goals of a 6 percent increase in annual purchasing power.

He was intrigued by the possible return on gold, but he was concerned with the projected 25 percent increase in price. He decided he had no feeling of whether it would rise or fall. All he had to go on was the opinion of the commodity broker. He concluded he would exclude gold from his investment alternatives.

Thus, through the process of elimination, he was left with common stocks and real estate. He reviewed his assumptions for each. He felt comfortable with his stock assumptions, but some of those he used for real estate bothered him. He talked to several landlords in the area and found that they experienced frequent turnover of tenants and that a better estimate would be ten months of rental per year. They also felt his upkeep figures could be too low and $1,600 would be a better estimate. He recomputed his projection using these two changed estimates and found he would actually lose money over the five-year projection.

He decided he would go with stocks, the investment alternative with which he felt most confident. He reviewed his financial analysis of XYZ Corporation once again and computed his return if the PE ratio remained at eight. He determined that he would still receive a 12.87 percent after-tax return, which would give him an increase of 5.8 percent in purchasing power.

George decided he should diversify his investments, so he began searching for three other stocks which he thought would have the same growth potential as XYZ Corporation. He would invest approximately $5,000 in each.

PART 4: ADVISORY SERVICES

You may wish to receive help in making your investment decisions. There are a wide range of services available to assist you in selecting investments. You can, if you wish, choose to have someone take complete charge of your investments. You should be very careful as to which services you select. Your investment needs are unique. They depend on your age, marginal tax bracket, the size and diversification of your investment portfolio, the impact inflation will have on your economic security, and many other factors. Unfortunately, few advisory services will take the time, or the interest, to properly understand your individual investment needs. Futhermore, many advisory services are compensated by charging you for each investment transaction. Some may be motivated to "churn" your account (frequent buying and selling of investments) in order to increase their earnings. Others tend to sensationalize their advice. They hope to gain attention and increase the sale of their services. Again, their objective may be to make money for themselves rather than for you.

We will first discuss some of the more typical advisory services that are available and then the criteria for determining which services you may wish to use.

MUTUAL FUNDS

If you invest in a mutual fund, you turn your investment capital over to the fund and have investment managers making the investment decisions. To join some funds you pay a sales commission. A charge of eight percent of your invested funds is typical. In addition, a charge is levied for the management of the fund's assets, and this charge is deducted from any income of the fund. A load fund charges a sales commission, while a no-load fund has no initial charge for investing. In either case, the managers of the fund expect to be compensated for their efforts. The net result is that your earnings on your investment are reduced by the sales and administrative costs incurred by the fund.

There are many different types of funds. A growth fund is primarily oriented to the purchasing of stocks that have appreciation potential, and the objective is to produce capital gains. An income fund's objective is to produce income. A balanced fund attempts to accomplish both. Many funds have a stated intent to invest in a particular type of industry, such as chemical, high technology, or energy. Others invest only in foreign securities. Some invest in corporate bonds, while others invest only in tax-free municipal bonds.

Some mutual funds belong to a so-called family of funds. They have a provision that you can move from fund to fund within the family of funds without a charge. This permits flexibility so that you can invest in a growth fund during a period in which you anticipate a rising stock market, move to a bond fund if you anticipate declining interest rates, and perhaps move to a money market fund when the future is uncertain and you wish to maintain a high liquidity.

If you elect to use a mutual fund for all, or a portion, of your investments, the primary task you face is to select the fund, or family of funds, with which you wish to entrust your dollars. There are services that rate the historical performance of all mutual funds. *Forbes Magazine*, for example, once a year rates all funds by comparing their performance against all other funds' results and against the change in stock market indices. The rating compares the results during both rising and falling markets. Some funds perform well during a rising market but perform poorly during down markets. You must decide what your investment objectives are and then which fund gives you the best opportunity to meet those objectives.

STOCK AND BOND BROKERS

A full-service stocks and bonds broker sells many investment alternatives in addition to stocks and bonds. Many of the larger firms provide advisory service and sell many types of limited partnerships, money market funds, life insurance annuities, and other investment alternatives. A full-service broker will have specialists who follow economic and stock market trends. They make recommendations on which individual stocks they perceive as having the best probability for appreciation. They recover the costs of providing this service in the commissions they charge for buying or selling your selected investment.

Discount brokers restrict their services to the handling of the purchase or sale of stocks and thus can charge a lower sales commission.

The value of the transactions generated determines the salesman's earnings. Thus it is understandable that few salesmen are interested in spending a lot of nonproductive time with a small investor. Some are not qualified to correctly identify your best investment strategy and make appropriate recommendations. Since commissions vary between the type of transaction (e.g., stocks vs. bonds), the salesman may also have a conflict between recommending what is best for you and what is best for them. You must consider all of these facts when you select a broker and a salesman to assist you in your investments.

MARKET LETTERS AND FINANCIAL PUBLICATIONS

There are numerous market letters to which you can subscribe. Many of the authors boast of past successes in predicting market turns and direction and specific investments that are going to be the best performers. Some attempt to become financial gurus by loudly proclaiming that theirs is the only true vision of the future. If they have made some correct past predictions, they may obtain a sizeable following. This usually lasts until they glaringly fail to predict a change in the direction of the market. Then a new prophet emerges and attempts to proselytize the former's disciples. One always wonders if the authors are primarily concerned with obtaining fees for their services to increase their income.

There are, however, many many good, reputable financial publications. They are too numerous and too varied to be covered fully here. The *Wall Street Journal, Barrons, Fortune, Forbes, Value*

Line, and many other sources will bring you knowledge that will greatly assist you in making your market decisions.

INVESTMENT COUNSELORS

Investment counselors are individuals who work with you on a one-on-one basis. They either advise on which investments to make, or they take charge of your investment portfolio and make the investment decisions. Their knowledge and competence vary widely. Some hope to make their money by the charges they assess against your investments for the transaction they make. Others charge you a percentage of the value of your investments as a management charge. If their fee is on a transaction basis, there is always the possibility of a conflict of interest, as they may generate numerous transactions to increase their income.

TAX ATTORNEYS, ACCOUNTANTS, BANKERS

For many investment alternatives, the tax code and accounting methods are complex, and the advice of a professional is a must. The fee for the attorney and the accountant will be based upon the time devoted to the research required to enable them to give you advice. I strongly urge that you develop a relationship with this type of professional as you begin to consider investment opportunities in more complex ventures. If you choose to use leverage in some of your investments, a good relationship with your banker is desirable.

TRUSTS

For a fee, your bank will set up a trust which will take your assets and manage them. If you have a sizeable portfolio but do not have the time or desire to manage your investments, this alternative has merit. It has merit at any stage of your life, but as you enter retirement it has increasing importance. The elderly are the favorite prey for swindlers and charlatans. If your spouse is not an informed investor, your death may be an invitation for unscrupulous individuals to cheat you out of your assets.

Unfortunately some may find that age will bring a diminished mental ability. They may not recognize, or care to admit, their diminished capacity. A trust administered for your benefit assures that your assets will be protected in your later years.

CRITERIA FOR PICKING ADVISORS

You may want to use several types of advisory services. But your chance of making a good selection will be greatly enhanced if you have developed your own knowledge and understanding of investment alternatives and strategies. My recommendation is that you give considerable thought to the selection of advisors and use the same method and care you would in selecting your personal physician. The following are some of the questions you should ask yourself:

- What training and experience do they have?
- Are they good listeners?
- Do they take the time to become informed of your investment goals, present investments, marginal tax rate, willingness to take risks, and long-range investment goals?
- Are they good communicators? Do they try to help and inform you, or are they primarily interested in impressing you?
- Are your personalities compatible?
- How are their services evaluated by existing clients?
- How do their results compare to that of other managers of investment funds?
- Does the compensation for their service have conflicts-of-interest implications?

Make the best selection you can, and if you make a mistake, don't be reluctant to admit it and seek help elsewhere.

SUMMARY

Most of us will need income from investments during retirement to live a satisfying life style. Few receive formal training on how to make investments. We must, therefore, obtain the necessary knowledge on our own. We need to become familiar with the various investment alternatives and obtain the knowledge and ability necessary to formulate an investment strategy designed to meet our unique financial needs. Two of the greatest deterrents to profitable investing are inflation and income taxes. We must keep the effect of these in mind as we consider investment alternatives and attempt to achieve purchasing power rewards.

In the early part of our careers we need to develop the habit of budgeting and saving. We should also begin our acquisition of knowledge about investments. Our first investments should be conservative in nature for the following reasons:

1. Our knowledge of investing is probably limited.
2. If the first investment finds us losing all or a part of our investment dollars, we are apt to become discouraged.
3. Early investments have the advantage of time and compounding, resulting in substantial increases in asset value.

Term life insurance and the purchase of a home should be among the first expenditures you consider. If possible, the next considerations should be an IRA plus account, company payroll savings, and stock purchase plan. If you have sufficient savings you may wish to consider more risky investments. A mutual fund might be an excellent choice.

By your mid-career years you should have acquired a good knowledge about investments. Your investment portfolio should be growing in both dollar value and diversification. Your income has probably reached the level where an increasing amount of your salary is going for income taxes. Prepare for this by learning how to allow the government to share a part of the risk of your investments. You also should understand the use of leverage and its application to your investment strategy.

Late-career years are usually the time you can really begin to build your investment assets. Family expenses will be decreasing, and you can invest a larger portion of your income. Your marginal tax rate will be high, and you can make risk investments that have the potential for a good purchasing power reward. Your knowledge of investment strategy should be mature. All the efforts of your early and mid-career years begin to bear fruit. With greater diversification, you can afford to take risks which in some cases should bring sizeable rewards. If you do pick a loser, it isn't going to destroy your portfolio.

As you approach retirement you should adopt a more conservative investment strategy again. If you have been successful with your investment plan to date, you should have ample funds to meet retirement needs. Your marginal tax rate will probably decrease after retirement, and some of your early high-risk investments are no longer suitable investment alternatives. With a reduced retirement income, any dollars lost through risk investments will be difficult to replace. Therefore, upon retirement you should recognize your changed investment environment and reshape your investment strategy.

Armed with the information contained in this chapter you can develop an investment strategy. Start now by completing WS-I.5.1 located in the appendix. Acquire additional knowledge to improve your investment skills. To be successful, apply diligence and patience. Learn from both your successes and failures. A successful investment strategy will improve the quality of your retirement.

Chapter 6

Contingency and Alternative Plans

Contingency and Alternate Plans

Your financial plan will not materialize exactly as projected. As time progresses, factors beyond your control change, requiring that you rethink and revise your basic plan. You may also find that through time your desires and wishes change.

Anticipate changes in the facts and assumptions you have developed and allow yourself ample lead time to decide courses of action to take as a result of the change. You do this by developing contingency and alternate plans.

CONTINGENCY PLANS

A contingency plan recognizes that some assumptions about future events will be incorrect. By making additional assumptions, you determine the effect these changed assumptions would have on your basic plan. The following are some of the changes you may wish to use in the construction of one or more of your contingency plans:

Inflation

Different rates of inflation will have a major impact on your basic financial plan. While you have assumed a certain inflation rate, no one knows for sure the future rates of inflation. You may wish to select one or more additional rates of inflation and make your financial projections using these inflation assumptions.

Longevity

With improvements in medicine we can expect that retirees will be living longer. The exhaustion of your financial resources in the final years of your retirement would be tragic. So you may wish to determine the effects of a longer life on your financial viability.

Promotions

You may have computed your pension anticipating that you will receive one or more promotions. Or, although you may not have planned on a promotion, you may receive one. Thus, you may wish to develop one or more contingency plans using different possibilities of promotion.

Health

You probably assumed good health at retirement and envisioned your desired retirement life style accordingly. You may want to develop a contingency plan assuming that your health at retirement will prevent your engaging in certain activities and determine how this change would affect your basic financial plan.

Income Taxes and Investments

You probably assumed that tax rates and policies would remain the same and that your investments would realize certain after-tax returns. As this is being written there is much discussion about making major changes in our federal income tax laws. For example, there has been some discussion of disallowing deductions for state income taxes. Such a change could have significant effect on your basic plan, and you may wish to prepare one or more contingency plans assuming different tax and investment assumptions.

Inheritance

Some of you have planned on receiving an inheritance, and you used these assets in the building of your basic plan. You may wish to determine the effect of either a larger or smaller inheritance.

Death

If you are married, the death of a spouse will alter significantly the basic financial plan for the survivor. Both income and expense will undoubtedly change. If only one spouse receives a pension and no survivor provisions have been selected, the surviving member may have a serious financial problem. A contingency plan should be developed to determine the financial viability of either member using the assumption that the other precedes him or her in death. A part of this plan should include a review of wills, trusts, and inheritance taxes.

ALTERNATE PLANS

You will recall that in the construction of your plan you developed and used several items we labeled facts. At some future date you may wish to change one or more of these planning inputs. An alternate plan is a change of plan caused by your choice, rather than a change dictated by external circumstances. The following are some of the alternate plans you may wish to consider:

Retirement Age

In your early or mid-career years, you are probably unsure just when you would like to retire. Many individuals experience career stress and/or "burn-out" in their late fifties and early sixties and, if they were financially able, would select early retirement. Others may presently feel they would like to retire early but, as the time approaches, find they would prefer to continue working. The current trend appears to be to allow individuals to continue to work at least until they are seventy. You may wish to develop alternate plans to determine your anticipated financial situation at one or more optional retirement ages, in addition to the one you selected in your basic plan.

Retirement Life Style

You may find that the costs of your desired retirement budget delays your retirement or that your ability to save and invest limits your desired retirement activities. You may wish to develop alternate plans varying your costs of retirement or your savings and investment program to determine if you have options not found in your basic plan.

Retirement Housing

One of your major costs of retirement will be housing. The money invested in or spent on retirement housing is not available for supporting other desires, such as traveling. You may find your preferences as to the type, size, or location of your planned retirement housing will change as you near retirement. By developing one or more alternate plans, you can determine the financial impact of different housing options on your financial plan.

Many considerations demonstrate the wisdom of preparing alternative or contingency plans. Obviously, developing plans to take care of every eventuality is not practical. Nonetheless, each of you should develop a list of major concerns and determine which could have the most serious impact on your financial future. Then select two or three that you feel are the most important and develop contingency and alternate plans, outlining how you propose to meet that eventuality. At this time complete WS-I.6.1.

Dealing With An Investment Deficit

Upon completing your basic plan covered in Chapter 3, some of you may have found that you projected an investment deficit that you could not eliminate through a savings and investment program. You may also find that one or more of your alternate or contingency plans will cause a financial imbalance. Many people find it necessary to supplement their retirement income by holding part-time or full-time jobs. You probably know retirees who, for instance, sell real estate, consult, or work in the travel industry. Others sell the product of their craft or hobby. If such activities add to their enjoyment of life, it is beneficial that they continue to work. However, if the only purpose is to produce income, and they find their work boring or demeaning, much of the joy of retirement will be lost.

If you need or will need the income, with some thought and preparation you should be able to find activities that will produce the needed funds and also add to your enjoyment of retirement.

The earlier in life you inventory your skills and interests and begin to prepare yourself for the retirement activity with which you plan to augment your income, the better chance you have in finding the right activity for you.

Section II of this book discusses how to prepare yourself to assure that your life has a purpose during retirement. If, after reading this section and filling out the work sheets, you discover that you will need supplemental income in retirement, prepare the plan that will give you not only the greatest opportunity to obtain the needed funds but also a sense of satisfaction and accomplishment.

Estate Planning

No financial plan is complete without estate planning. Every estate plan should include a will, and many will find a trust advantageous.

Fifty percent of Americans die without a properly drawn and executed will. When this happens, the state in effect writes your will for you and thus dictates how your assets are divided among your heirs. In most instances this division will not be in accordance with the best interests of the recipients. For example, in many states the spouse will receive only a portion of the assets, and the balance will be divided among the children. Thus the first effort in estate planning is to prepare a will with the help of a good attorney. It is never too early to prepare a will even though you may have limited assets.

A properly drawn will conserves assets, minimizes taxes, and arranges for the distribution of your assets, including any special bequests.

Often a trust is a desirable part of a good estate plan. The primary uses of trusts are

- To provide competent management of funds left to a spouse (Either because of age or incompetence, the survivor may not be skilled in handling financial resources.)
- To reduce state inheritance taxes and federal estate taxes
- To require that your assets be used in a particular way after you are gone
- To provide for management of your funds if you should become incompetent because of diminished mental or physical vigor

The drawing of a will and the preparing of trusts are the job of a professional. You should not attempt to do either on your own. The various state laws and federal regulations are so complex that you should always employ the services of an expert.

It is a good idea to become aware of the various possibilities and the basic principles of estate planning prior to seeing at attorney. You can accomplish this by attending seminars, reading material obtained from your library, and talking to friends who have completed their estate planning. This will enable you and the attorney to spend your time more productively during your first meeting. At the very least, you should have an up-to-date net worth statement, an agreement with your spouse on how each of you want the estate handled, the names and addresses of all beneficiaries, and a list of any items you wish to pass to friends or children. Your estate plan should be reviewed and, if necessary, updated

- Any time you move to a new state
- If any significant change occurs in pertinent state or federal laws

- If a significant change occurs in the value of assets
- If you or your spouse change your mind on how you wish to distribute the assets
- If you wish to change the individual or institution named to be the administrator of your estate and/or trust
- At the time of your retirement

Peace of mind and the knowledge that your loved ones will be taken care of are important, especially in your retirement years. The investment of time and money to assure your affairs are in order is well spent. Estate planning is not a matter that should be put off until tomorrow.

Chapter 7

Monitoring Progress

Monitoring Progress

If you don't know where you are, you are lost; and if you don't know where you are going, any road will get you there.

By now you should know where you are. You have determined your net worth, and you have developed facts and assumptions. You also know where you are going: You are going to arrive at retirement with adequate financial resources. Your financial plan is your road map to prescribe the route. But, like every trip, arriving at your destination requires that you implement your plan. The implementation requires effort and self-discipline. Occasionally you will backslide and get off the indicated path. The way to assure you get back on track is to periodically monitor your progress.

ANNUAL INVENTORY

I would suggest that at least once a year you take inventory of how you are doing. The preparation of an annual net worth statement will indicate the progress you have made. Review the rest of your facts and assumptions. Perhaps your views or interests will have changed during the past year. Consult with your spouse to be sure you still have the same thoughts about the style of retirement you desire, the location and type of housing you prefer, the outlook for inflation, and all the other considerations you used in preparing your basic plan. Review you skills and interests. Perhaps you have acquired new interests or skills which you may want to use in your planning.

Take a look at your budget and determine how inflation has impacted your living costs over the past year. You will probably find that your actual costs increased at a different rate than the Consumer Price Index. You may wish to use your personalized consumer price index for future cost projections.

ANNUAL UPDATE

After completing these preliminaries, update your plan for the coming and subsequent years by following the format outlined in Chapters 1 through 5.

Next review Chapter 6 on Investment Alternatives and Strategies. Ask yourself the following questions:

- Did I obtain my objectives?
- Is my balanced risk line the same as last year?
- Did I obtain the planned investment knowledge during the past year?
- Should I continue the same investment strategy during the coming year?

Then prepare the coming year's investment plan and decide how to increase your knowledge of investments.

Don't be discouraged if you did not obtain all of your objectives and goals during the past year. Simply resolve to do better during the coming year.

Following these suggestions takes time. There will be no harm in doing a little at a time and spreading the process over several months. Establish a schedule of sequencing through the process. For example, you may wish to look at your net worth the first two weeks in January, examine the facts and assumptions the last two weeks, update your basic plan during the month of February, develop your coming year's investment strategy during the month of March, and update alternative and contingency plans in April. By using this method you will never feel rushed or burdened by the undertaking. You may find the process stimulating and rewarding. Each year, as you cycle through the exercise, you will find it easier to complete.

Again, do not become overly concerned if you get off the road occasionally. As long as you know your destination and the road that will take you there, you have a good plan. Use the annual checkup to find out where you have strayed from the path, and take action to correct your deviations. Have confidence that you are going to arrive at your destination (your golden years) with financial security.

KEEPING THE PROPER PERSPECTIVE

Before we leave this section on financial planning, there are some thoughts I would like to leave with you.

Your plan deals with averages over the period of your plan. For example, you assumed a certain earning power for your assets. We know that we have economic cycles and the earning power of your investments will probably fluctuate in accordance with these cycles. If over some periods your earnings do not measure up to your expectations, you may become discouraged and either start to speculate rather than invest, or abandon your savings program. Maintain a long-term perspective as you evaluate your progress.

There is a danger that some will make the acquiring of money the central focus of their lives. The possession of money does not bring happiness. You will recall that in the introduction I stated that a successful retirement requires three ingredients, namely, (1) financial security, (2) life with a purpose, and (3) good health. I consider financial security to be the least important of the three. It does, however, facilitate acquiring the other two.

Every individual should feel that his or her life has a purpose. Life with a Purpose will be explored in the next section of this book. A retirement with sufficient income will allow you to devote your time to activities of your choice without the distraction of time spent simply to earn a living.

SECTION II:
Life With a Purpose

Chapter 1—The Rites of Passage....................113
Chapter 2—On Becoming a Retiree................119
Chapter 3—Reach Out and Touch Someone....129
Chapter 4—The Gap is the Problem...............137
Chapter 5—Who am I?...................................143
Chapter 6—Why am I?..................................157
Chapter 7—How?...171

Chapter 1

The Rites of Passage

The Rites of Passage

Our lives consist of many stages or phases. Leaving one stage and entering into the next requires change: change in our values, change in the way we use our time, and change in the way we relate to others. By the time we become a candidate for retirement, we have passed through several stages of life. Some of the major transitions we have made are

- From the sanctuary of the home to a competitive school environment
- From the academic environment to the economic world
- From individual responsibility to a marital union
- From being without children to being parents

HISTORICAL RITES OF PASSAGE

Not everyone adapts easily to new roles. Throughout history, therefore, society has attempted to assist individuals in their transition from one phase to the next by establishing rites of passage. These rites instruct the person on what is expected of them as they adjust to their new roles. In some instances, the ritual or ceremony contains the information. In others, the expectations of society are understood and communicated. Some rites are very specific, and the litany is dictated by the church or state.

Some of the significant rites of passage are show below:

RITE OF PASSAGE	TRANSITION
Bar Mitzvah (boy)	
Bat Mitzvah (girl)	Young Adulthood
Debutante Ball (girl)	
Graduation	Completion of Formal Education
Marriage Vows	Marriage
Christening or Baptism	Religious Commitment
Funeral	Death

Retirement also has its rite of passage — the retirement party. But it is of recent origin and does not benefit from centuries of experience.

THE LENGTHENING LIFE SPAN AND FINANCIAL INDEPENDENCE

Only during the latter part of this century has a large segment of our society had the opportunity to retire. Longevity and financial independence are of recent origin. Throughout history, including the early part of this century, the few individuals whose life span continued into their sixth or seventh decade often remained a part of their family unit and relied on this unit for their physical needs. Three-generation families in one household constituted a typical retirement arrangement. The grandparent continued to perform services for the unit, even if on an ever-diminishing scale (due to failing physical or mental abilities). Our largely rural and agrarian society could always use an extra hand to provide for the necessities of the family unit, even if the contribution was limited by the infirmities of age.

Modern medicine and improved health habits have dramatically increased the average life span of our population. Most people can now anticipate reaching their later years of life with undiminished mental abilities and good physical vigor.

The urbanization of our society has altered the utility of a three-generation family unit. Furthermore, today a four-generation family is not at all unusual.

In summary, society finds itself with an increasing number of its members achieving retirement, and it has limited experience in helping them make the necessary transition. So, we should not be surprised that the rite of passage associated with retirement (the retirement party) gives little help in preparing the retiree for his or her new role in life.

THE RETIREMENT PARTY'S IMPLIED MESSAGE

The message conveyed by the rite associated with retirement does more harm than good. Let's reflect on the social message conveyed by the typical retirement party. The program usually consists of an assembling of friends and associates and the presenting of one or more speeches extolling the retiring individual for the contributions made to the welfare of their organization, their family, and the community. The format is very similar to the eulogies that will be given at their funeral. A part of the message conveyed is that the person being honored deserves the leisure and hedonistic activities that one assumes will characterize their retirement life style. The unspoken assumption is that the retiree's declining physical and mental capacity has lessened his or her value as a contributing member to the welfare of their organization and society.

The eulogies are traditionally followed by the presenting of gifts. Golf clubs, fishing and hunting equipment, and luggage are some of the typical gifts. The message is again given that the expected ultimate concern of the retiree will be the pursuit of fun and games. The retiree is then asked to say a few words. The gist of the message is a statement of their appreciation for the support and friendship of all their associates and a promise that they will keep in touch. Everyone knows the retiree is being separated from the inner circle, and while there may be an occasional phone call and Christmas card, the past interpersonal relationships will be dramatically altered. Everyone hopes that "good old Joe" will not be one of those who frequently drops by the office to discuss the glories of the past while they are trying to cope with the crises of the present. The feeling pervades the gathering that they are here to pay homage to an individual that is "over the hill."

As stated previously, the purpose of a rite of passage is to give the participant instructions on the expectations of society as he or she assumes a new role. The graduation exercise extols the graduate to go out into the world and be productive to make it a better place. The marriage ceremony includes an exchange of vows by the participants. They promise to nurture and support each other, with the thought that the merging of their lives will create a union that is stronger than either would be functioning independently. The christening calls for the nurture and support of the newborn by the assembled congregation. On the other hand, the retirement ceremony advises retirees to get lost and enjoy their life of fun and games. It is assumed that their productive years are behind them.

That is what society expects, but is society wrong? Society lacks sufficient experience with an older population to convey the proper instructions.

PLANNING FOR CHANGE

As we entered each new stage of life, we were required to make certain changes and adaptations. As we left childhood, we had to change. Marriage required change. The birth of children brought further change. Retirement will require that we change. Not everyone makes the changes required to pass successfully from one stage of life to the next. We all know individuals whose lives have been tragic because of the inability, or unwillingness, to make the necessary transitional changes.

The purpose of this section on Life with a Purpose is to give you some thoughts and options for planning to make the changes required if you are to have a successful retirement. Be assured that, if you make the effort, retirement can be the high point of your life, rather than the beginning of the end.

Chapter 2

On Becoming a Retiree

On Becoming a Retiree

It is normal to be somewhat apprehensive about the unknown. As we make the transition from one phase of our life to the next, we experience anxieties because we cannot predict our ability to cope with required changes. Understanding and planning for the necessary changes eases the trauma of the transition. We will attempt to do just that in the remaining chapters in this section.

We are each unique and different, so only general methods of achieving introspection and self-analysis will be suggested for your use in arriving at a better understanding of yourself. However, we all have certain physical and emotional needs in common. Our satisfaction with life depends on the methods we employ in using our unique abilities and skills to satisfy these universal needs.

In this chapter we will concentrate on these universal needs. Subsequent chapters will focus on methods for identifying your uniqueness and for using your skills to achieve a life with a purpose in your retirement years.

Behavioral scientists have identified certain needs and the actions we take to satisfy these needs. Unfortunately, little use of this knowledge has been applied to retirement. The primary use has been in business and industry to improve employee job satisfaction and productivity. We will attempt to take some of their findings and apply them to the retirement phase of life.

THE HIERARCHY OF NEEDS

Abraham Maslow, one of the pioneers in behavioral science, suggests that people have a hierarchy of needs. Until a need is filled, the higher needs do not come into play; once a need is filled, the next need in the hierarchy becomes dominant.

His ranking of these needs is as follows, starting with the lowest and continuing to the highest:

1. Physiological   The need to sustain life itself: food, shelter, and clothing
2. Safety or Security The need for self-preservation, both now and in the future
3. Social or Affiliation The desire for meaningful relationships with others
4. Esteem   The need for self-esteem and the esteem of others
5. Self-Actualization The need to maximize our potential

Let's look at each of these five needs and try to understand how they may affect our satisfaction with life in our retirement years.

Physiological Needs

Fortunately, only a very small segment of the retired population find themselves unable to obtain adequate food, clothing, or shelter. Various social agencies and assistance programs are available for those without the means to provide for these most basic needs. However, to find yourself reduced to mere survival, in what should be your best years of life, is certainly a tragedy.

Safety and Security

Many retirees are very concerned about their financial security. While they are able to provide for their physiological needs today, inflation, rising energy and medical costs, and a fixed income foretells a future in which they will be unable to provide the basic necessities of life for themselves. Frequently this situation is one of their own making. Improper and imprudent financial planning in their earlier years has led to their present predicament. It was not by accident that the first section of this book dealt with financial planning.

Physical security is also a major concern of many retirees. Their vulnerability to robbery, mugging, and physical harm is well documented on television and in the newspapers. The careful selection of the retirement community and the perimeter protection of their dwelling unit can provide a needed sense of security. Emergency-alert systems and a buddy system of daily contact can quiet a troubled mind concerned that a sudden illness will leave one alone and helpless. Careful attention to in-home hazards (such as stairs and bath tubs) can prevent debilitating accidents that could render an individual helpless and dependent.

Once one has taken all prudent security precautions, mental attitude becomes extremely important. A vivid imagination can conjure up all sorts of tragic scenarios. An active physical and intellectual life style will lessen the safety concerns.

Social or Affiliation Needs

For some retirees the first difficulty in retirement will be finding ways to satisfy their social needs. Retirees may make the decision either to continue to live in their preretirement community or to move to a new community. Both present problems. If you decide to stay in the same community and most of your friends are still active in their business or profession, you may find that your interests slowly change, and your present relationships may gradually cool, with the result that you are lonely. Conversely, you may move to a new location and find difficulty in making new friends. Many who select retirement communities believe the opportunity to associate with other retirees will lead to friends with the same interests and values. Some are satisfied with their associations, but others find the relationships sterile and depressing. Many retirees are self-centered and tend to live in the past. Exclusive association with such people stymies intellectual growth. The next chapter in this section explores our social needs in more depth and offers thoughts concerning courses of action to satisfy this need.

Esteem

Our esteem needs consist of our needs for self-esteem and the esteem of others. The loss of esteem is frequently a major detractor from a satisfying retirement. Some people require the approval of others before they can approve of themselves. Your opinion of your worth as a human being can be entirely independent of others' opinion of you. Conversely, it is also true that others tend to view you as you view yourself. If you like yourself (in a nonoffensive way), others will tend to like you. If you think of yourself as an "over-the-hill has-been," others will probably perceive you in the same way. It behooves preretirees to engage in some serious introspection and, if necessary, change their self-esteem needs to better serve their retirement years. Chapter 4 offers some thoughts on how you may accomplish this.

Self-Actualization

Our self-actualization needs are the most difficult to identify and define. Our ultimate concern or concerns are individualistic and complex. To complicate the matter further, few of us can articulate the need for self-actualization. At best we have a general feeling as to whether we are satisfied with what we are doing with our life. For those preretirees who have a sense of satisfaction with their life, the pertinent question is, "Will my retirement activities give me the same sense of satisfaction?" The early years of adulthood were spent acquiring the tools and means to satisfy our basic physiological needs. We later progressed to satisfying our security, social, and self-esteem needs. Many find themselves locked in a vocation and life style that fails to fulfill their needs for self-actualization. With careful planning, this group should be able to direct their resources and activities in such a manner that, perhaps for the first time in their lives, they have the opportunity to fulfill their self-actualization needs, and for the first time, believe their life has a purpose. Subsequent chapters in this section suggest methods of engaging in needed introspection and planning to enhance the probability that your retirement years will bring a purpose to life.

MOTIVATION FACTORS

Frederick Herzberg, another behavioral scientist, has done extensive research on motivation. He reached the conclusion that certain job-related environmental factors can be classified as HYGIENE items. If these factors are absent, the individual will be unhappy in his or her work. If these factors are present, the individual will be happy, but may not necessarily feel motivated. He found that if other conditions were present, the individual would feel happy, motivated, and enthusiastic about his or her life and job. The table below lists these factors:

HYGIENE FACTORS (job environment)	MOTIVATORS (the job itself)
Policies and Administration	Achievement
Supervision	Recognition
Working conditions	Challenging work
Interpersonal relations	Increasing responsibility
Money, status, security	Growth and development

Let's compare Maslow's and Herzberg's findings as shown in the following table.

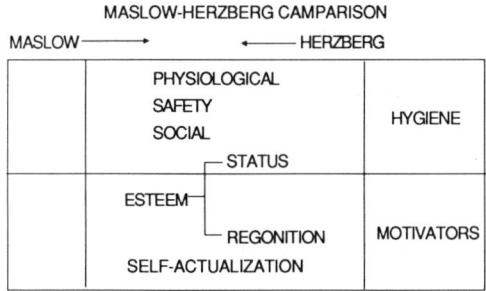

You will note that they agree. Herzberg expands on Maslow's findings and states that our physiological, safety, security, and status needs must be fulfilled for us to be happy. He labels these as *hygiene needs*. He further states that we need to have our recognition and self-actualization needs met to feel motivated. He labels these needs as *motivators*.

Status

Status is our position or ranking in a social structure. *Where does the retiree rank?* Each of us has a perception as to where we think we should rank, and our feeling of self-worth is influenced by our perception of how we are ranked by society.

Recognition and Self-Actualization

Recognition is earned by ourselves and granted by others as a result of our competence and achievement. *What are the retiree's accomplishments and achievements?*

To summarize, Herzberg found that for you to be happy on your job, the hygiene factors, namely; pay, security, social needs, and status must be present. To be motivated you need recognition and the feeling that you are doing challenging work and experiencing personal development.

MEETING OUR NEEDS IN RETIREMENT

Using these findings, we can predict that if certain conditions are present, we will be content in our retirement. If additional conditions are present, we will have a zest for life. That is, we will face each new day with the feeling that the best is yet to be. The following table lists the conditions:

CONTENTMENT WITH RETIREMENT	ZEST FOR LIFE
• Satisfaction with retirement location • Sufficient financial resources to sustain our desired life style • Marital harmony • Circle of friends and acquaintances • Good self-image	• Challenging and meaningful activities and hobbies • Appreciation by friends and family • Intellectual stimulation • Perception of making a contribution to society

Each of us can study the above model and gain insight into what conditions should be present if we are to be satisfied and excited about our retirement phase of life. We can classify ourselves as:

- *Unhappy* with our retirement (We lack the hygiene factors.)
- *Content*, but without a zest for life (We have the hygiene or contentment factors but not those creating zest in our lives.)
- *Having zest for life* (We have the contentment factors and at least most of those needed for a zest for life.)

The following diagram displays the various ways we perceive our lives, both before and after retirement.

```
PRERETIREMENT LIFE STYLE     RETIREMENT LIFE STYLE

              TRANSITIONS

   UNHAPPY ─────┐         ┌──── UNHAPPY
   HAPPY ───────┼───▶─────┼──── HAPPY
   MOTIVATED ───┘         └──── ZEST FOR LIFE
```

Our satisfaction with retirement will be dependent upon the degree of change we experience between our preretirement life style, and our retirement life style. The unhappy preretiree who becomes an unhappy retiree may notice little change in their perception of the quality of their life. If they progress from a state of unhappiness to one of contentment, they will view retirement as an improvement.

Pity the individuals who found their jobs motivating but then find unhappiness in retirement. The degree of change causes them to experience a traumatic sense of loss.

Our goal should be a transition from whatever state we find ourselves in preretirement to one where we have a zest for life. It can be done, and the following chapters will tell you how.

Your first task is to evaluate how you feel about your present life style. WS-II.2.1 is provided to assist you in making this evaluation. Consider Herzberg's findings as you complete the work sheet.

Next predict how you will feel about retirement. Be as honest with yourself as possible. The time to recognize that you have some work to do to prepare yourself for retirement is now. Self-deception will only delay the time when these issues must be faced. Although it is difficult to predict future emotions, do the best you can. Give special attention to those questions which result in a *No* or *Don't Know* answer.

Then select the type of transition you believe is most likely for you, provided that you make no special effort to prepare yourself for retirement. And finally, document any thoughts you have on actions to better prepare you for the transition so that you will have a genuine zest for life.

Chapter 3

Reach Out and Touch Someone

Reach Out and Touch Someone

Our social needs are present with us from infancy. A baby that is deprived of interpersonal contacts will become neurotic and have an arrested emotional development. Young children have a strong desire to be a part of the group. All through our life we want to experience social intercourse. Most individuals will significantly modify their behavior pattern to obtain group approval.

THE NEED FOR SOCIAL INTERACTION

Thus it is not surprising that we will continue to have social needs in retirement. But in many instances, a significant change is required in where and how we satisfy these needs. We will want to join new groups in order to continue our social contacts.

Common interest is the cohesive force binding groups together. As our careers progress, most of us find that the demands of our jobs, positions, or professions cause a decrease in the number of our outside interests. Our focus narrows and intensifies — sometimes even at the expense of our relationship with our spouse and family. For many preretirees their primary, and in some cases their only, social group is business associates.

Retirement separates the retiree from this group; and unless other sources of acquaintances and friends are found, the loss of opportunities for social interaction can be traumatic.

Frequently, new retirees concentrate all their social needs on their spouse, and the recipient feels smothered. The oft-quoted lament of the wife of a newly retired individual of "twice as much husband with half the income" is humorous because of the relevancy.

The retiree with limited interests who chooses to move to a new location further compounds the problem.

ENHANCING SOCIAL SKILLS

A healthy social relationship has both quantity and quality dimensions. One should have a sizeable number of acquaintances and several friends. Most people would also like to have a few close friends. A close friend is someone we fully accept in spite of their faults and who fully accepts us in spite of our shortcomings. The relationship doesn't encourage us to pretend we are something we are not (we don't have to wear masks) and both feel their life is enriched by the association.

Developing Multiple Interests

After retirement, we can no longer count on our business associates to provide for our social needs, so we must look to other groups to provide us with a sizeable number of acquaintances. To increase our opportunities to make new friends, we should develop a variety of interests.

An individual or a couple who are interested in golf, belong to a country club, participate in the activities of a religious organization, belong to a dance group, play bridge, and do volunteer work at the hospital will have a great number of acquaintances.

Turning Acquaintances into Friends

The next step is to upgrade some of those acquaintances into friendships. This is more difficult than it first appears. Too often we use the hard-sell approach. We become acquainted with someone we would like to know better and attempt to convince them that we are intelligent, witty, important — someone worth having as a friend. If they too are interested in promoting the relationship, they are rehearsing their sale's pitch while we are talking. At the first break in the conversation, they begin their sale's pitch. Neither party really listens and, finally, after a mutually unsuccessful attempt at communication, each leaves with a sigh of relief and a feeling of gratitude that "I finally got away from the self-centered bore."

Improving Communication Skills

In the process of making friends it is important that we have or develop communication skills. The following are but a few of the techniques to become a better listener and communicator.

Effective Listening The skill of understanding listening is almost a must if you wish to acquire genuine friends. Like most skills, understanding listening requires knowledge and execution. We can listen much more rapidly than we can speak, so our minds wander while another is talking. And as our minds wander, we often lose important portions of the speaker's thoughts. Effective listening requires concentration on what the other person is saying. Concentration requires effort and energy.

Body Language Considerable communication takes place through kinesics or body language. We have all experienced attempting to converse with an individual whose body language indicated that they were not receptive to our communications. If an individual's body language and verbal communications are conveying different messages, we tend to become confused and sometimes irritated.

Semantics Another problem hindering effective communications is semantics. Words are an imperfect means of expressing thoughts or ideas. The speaker attempts to convey a thought through the use of words. Those words may well create a different thought or concept in the mind of the listener. If the listener is genuinely interested in understanding the concept the speaker is attempting to convey, several attempts to express the thought may be required before an approximation of the understanding of an idea can be obtained.

Comprehension We have a tendency to hear what we want to hear and reject information we do not want to receive. I am sure you have experienced going to a meeting and subsequently discovering that the participants came away with widely differing concepts on what was said and the conclusions reached.

In order for meaningful dialogue to take place, the participants must have skills in speaking and listening. Considerable training is given on effective speaking. Few are trained to be good listeners. There are, however, books, seminars, and classes dealing with effective listening. Your ability to make and maintain friends in retirement will be enhanced if you choose to develop your listening skills.

Showing Interest in the Other Person

The greatest compliment you can pay an individual is to indicate that you are interested in them as an individual. Supportive remarks (such as "I see," "Tell me more," "That is interesting") encourage an individual to reach deeper into his or her individuality and begin to share with you some of his or her innermost being. You begin to know them better. If they, in turn, give you time to talk and give you their undivided attention, you are on the road to making a new friend. If they do not give you your turn, you are probably not interested in promoting the relationship anyway.

You will probably find that only a small percentage of your acquaintances will advance to the stage of a friend. From your circle of friends will emerge candidates for the position of close friend. The same listening techniques are applicable to the selection of these individuals. It is a rare occurrence when two personalities are so compatible that each feels "I'm OK - you're OK" and the relationship rises to the level of close friend. Most individuals consider themselves fortunate to have had a few close friends in their lifetime. The support of a friend in times of joy or adversity can greatly enhance the pleasure of the moment and turn an otherwise intolerable situation of adversity into one with which you can cope.

SOURCES FOR FRIENDSHIPS

We continually search for new candidates for the position of friend. This will require that we open the door for new possibilities.

Original Circle of Friends

One of the mistakes of many older people is that they do not continue to maintain their circle of acquaintances and friends. The ravages of time will decimate this circle, and unless care is taken to continuously add new members, the last years of life may well find them alone and lonely.

New Acquaintances

The advantages and disadvantages of retiring in the community where you lived just prior to retirement are many and varied, as we have discussed. If you have developed the interests and the abilities that will enable you to readily make acquaintances, friends, and close friends, you need not be concerned that a relocation will find you unable to fulfill your social needs.

Family

There is another source of friendship that I have left until last in our discussion — not because it is of lesser importance, but for the same reason we leave our dessert until the end of our meal. This friendship gives an added dimension to our life. I am referring to one's relationship with family, and especially one's spouse.

Probably you and your spouse had a best-friend relationship during your courtship and early marriage. The pressures of the job and preoccupation with children created a divergence of interests that increased over the years, and you came to take each other for granted. It may be that you rarely engage in meaningful communications. Retirement will give you the opportunity to renew the former relationship. The developing and sharing of common interests and the restoration of meaningful communications can once again promote your spouse to the status of best friend. Together, mutually supporting each other, you can face life's joys and sorrows with confidence and hope.

Perhaps for the first time your relationship with your children can be elevated from a parent-child relationship to that of friend. It is well worth the effort.

The relationship with grandchildren can be especially rewarding. You have the opportunity to once again enjoy all the joys of parenthood without the responsibilities. The kinship of a grandparent to a grandchild is special, and you can use some of your new-found time to enhance that relationship.

WS-II.3.1 asks you to engage in some self-analysis and also suggests that you evaluate your resources and skills for acquiring acquaintances and friends. If you determine that there are interests or abilities that you wish to acquire in order to improve your social skills, it is suggested you prepare a plan on ways to acquire the resources to enhance your social skills.

Chapter 4
The Gap is The Problem

The Gap is the Problem

If we have self-esteem, we approve of and like ourselves. The problems arise when there is a gap between what we perceive we should be and what we think we are. Many of us have a rather fragile sense of self-worth. We constantly look to others to give us clues. Our social system is filled with indicators. For example, industry and organizations have job titles that give quick and precise information of how the organization evaluates individuals. Titles such as "Doctor" immediately convey that the individual is someone of importance. Membership in the right club, a home in the right community, and the ownership of the right make of automobile are all methods society uses in identifying the individual's status in society.

RECOGNIZING THE GAP

When a significant gap exists between what a person thinks he should be and what he perceives he is, personality aberrations appear. The result may be an inferiority complex or a feeling of unworthiness. Such individuals often overcompensate. That is, they develop a myopic drive to acquire status symbols and the approval of others. To acquaintances, they appear egotistical and obnoxious. Some executives surround themselves with "yes-men" to assure that they receive constant feedback that tells them how great they are. In this way they support their fragile sense of self-worth.

The self-esteem drive is powerful and complex. If improperly channeled, it can create havoc in the lives of the individual, his or her family, and associates.

As previously stated, the problem is the gap. The solution is to narrow the gap. This can be accomplished by redefining who we are, or who we should be, or both.

Pete's Story

Maybe you can anticipate how retirement will affect your self-esteem. We will present a hypothetical individual and predict how retirement might affect his sense of self-worth. We meet him approximately a year before he retires and ask him "Pete, who are you?" He answers:

I am

- Vice President of A. B. C. Company (I am an important person with the title, office, and perks to prove it.)
- A boss with power (My subordinates follow my direction and tell me what a great guy I am in a variety of ways.)
- A person making an excellent salary (I belong to the right clubs, live in the right community, wear expensive clothes, and travel with the right crowd.)
- A good golfer (I have a membership in Gotrocks Country Club and have a 10 handicap.)
- A husband (That is my wife's picture on my desk. She is attractive and dresses well.)
- A father (Let me tell you how well my two sons are doing in their jobs. They take after me.)

Let's see how Pete will probably answer the same question one year after he retires.

I am

- A retired (a has-been) Vice President of A.B.C. Company (I used to be somebody.)
- A leader (But I have a lousy bunch of followers. I am President of my Country Club, but in spite of all my good work, all I hear are complaints from the members. I tried to tell my wife how she could organize her household chores to be more efficient, but she told me to "butt out.")
- Well-off financially (I take the right trips and tell my acquaintances at every opportunity about my brilliant investments.)
- A golfer (I belong to Shady Lane Country Club — I used to belong to Gotrocks. I have a 13 handicap — it used to be 10. I can't understand it because I play three times a week and I am really trying to improve. But the harder I try, the worse I get.)
- A husband (But my wife seems to resent my being around the house so much.)

- A father (My sons seem to be more interested in their jobs these days and don't seek my advice any longer.)

Is it possible that Pete's value as a human being has changed so dramatically in a short twenty-four months? He still has the same intelligence, talents, and skills. He remains essentially the same person he was prior to retirement. But his support system has changed. He no longer has a title, the office, or the clubs that clearly identified his status in society. People do not seem to be taking his advice anymore. His role in life has changed. He appears to have a self-esteem problem. He is trying to tie his present situation to the past in order to retain his prior sense of self-worth.

CLOSING THE GAP

Remember, self-esteem problems develop because of a gap between what we think we should be and what we perceive we are. We can close this gap by changing our perception of who we are, or who we would like to be, or both.

Prior to retirement, most individuals have several occasions in their lives when they experience the psychic pain brought about by the loss of self-esteem. Children leaving home, divorce, failure to get a promotion, loss of a job — all may result in a loss of self-esteem. If you experienced any of the above, you may recall the pain associated with the event and remember the effort you had to make to regain your self-respect and emotional health.

We all know of individuals who were star athletes in high school or college and who have spent the rest of their lives trying to recapture the status and recognition achieved from their athletic abilities. Others with equal fame accepted their period of recognition with grace and then moved on to achieve self-esteem in other ways.

As we have discussed, the loss of self-esteem brings pain. In addition it can result in health problems. All too often, healthy, vital individuals become listless and experience failing health soon after they retire. I hope that I have convinced you that it is to your benefit to evaluate how you presently perceive yourself and, if necessary, plan to make changes in your self-esteem needs before retirement.

Complete Section I, II, and IV of WS-II.4.1. Have your spouse (or a close friend) complete the appropriate portion of Section II. Use care in recording your answers. After you complete the form, review your answers to determine if they actually reflect who you feel you are. You may wish to change some of the wording as a result of the additional insight the review may bring. Continue the process until you are satisfied you have the best answers possible.

Ideally, the completion of WS-II.4.1, will provide you insight into "who you are." Subsequent chapters in this section will assist you in determining "who you should be."

Pete's New Value System

Let's assume our friend Pete spent some time on gaining insight into himself in preparation for retirement and see how he might now answer the question, "Who are you?"

I am

- An intelligent human with skills and knowledge. My company has recognized this by giving me a position of responsibility.
- A friend and advisor who enjoys working with my associates and takes pride in their accomplishments and promotions.
- A person who is fortunate to be financially independent and does not have to be concerned about having enough income to provide for the type of life style my wife and I enjoy. I am fortunate to be able to belong to a country club, have a nice home, and drive a nice car.
- A person who enjoys playing golf. I value the fellowships I have experienced as a result of belonging to a country club.
- A husband who is fortunate to have a wonderful person as my companion and friend.
- A father who is proud of his children and enjoys their friendship and the association with my grandchildren.

If Pete has been truthful in his answers, it is obvious he has changed his system of values. He appears to be less self-centered and more in control of his life. He is less dependent on others for his self-image. He is interested in meaningful relationships and, I would guess, a better listener.

I doubt that I would have liked to have the "old Pete" as a friend. But I would be interested in becoming better acquainted with the "new Pete."

Chapter 5
Who am I?

Who am I?

The happiest people are those who discover what they should be doing and who then do it. In other words, what they should be doing and what they are doing are the same thing.

What we should be doing depends upon (1) our stage in life, (2) our inherent and acquired talents and skills, and (3) the discovery of our proper role in a society that is rapidly changing and becoming increasingly complex.

As discussed in the first chapter of this section, society has had little experience in dealing with financially independent, healthy retirees, and so it offers incorrect clues to a suitable retirement life style.

If we trace the flow of life from birth to retirement and extrapolate, we can gain some thoughts as to suitable retirement roles.

We have also discussed the various stages of life and the transitions required. I would now like to approach the subject from a different perspective and see if this vista will help the retiree answer the question, "Who am I?" The stages of life we will discuss are typical for individuals who choose employment with a medium- to large-sized company. With this information, each of you can then construct a life style analysis for other vocations even though they may significantly differ from what is covered here.

TYPICAL ROLES

The phases we will analyze are explorer, provider, competitor, advisor, and reaper. Let's look at each.

Explorer

This stage begins at birth and usually continues into our early or mid-twenties. We are exploring the world of knowledge and preparing to take our place as a responsible adult in society. During this period, our physiological and safety needs are provided by our parents. During our earliest years, our acceptance and self-esteem needs are furnished by our family. As we begin our formal schooling, we seek to become a part of groups, and the need for acceptance becomes especially apparent in our early teens. We satisfy our self-esteem needs in a variety of ways. We may become a leader in our group, a jock, a good student, or a sought-after date with the opposite sex. We are torn between our desire to remain under the protection of our family and our need to become an independent and unique personality.

About the time we enter college we begin to struggle with Who am I? What should my life's work be, and What is the purpose for my life? Most individuals are idealistic during this period, but many must sacrifice their idealism for practicality. Their need to prepare themselves to become self-supporting necessitates that they compromise and select a course of study that will enable them to find employment and provide for their own financial needs. Some are unfortunate in that they choose a career that fails to give their life a purpose.

Provider

After we finish our formal education, we are expected to become productive members of society and to provide for our own financial needs. We package our acquired knowledge, skills, abilities, and talents and exchange them for money. Our choice of where we will work is influenced by our perceived and subliminal needs. For example, if we have high security needs (perhaps because of childhood experiences), we may elect to work for a large, stable organization or a government agency because we think that job will be secure.

Many individuals marry and have children early in their career and feel locked into their jobs, since they must provide for their family's physiological needs. Thus, some see their adolescent dreams and fantasies disappearing. They become disillusioned and adopt a survivor mentality.

Competitor

Most individuals want promotions in order to obtain additional income. They seek the increase in salary as a way of providing for more security and desired status symbols. Also a need for self-esteem creates drives to obtain positions of increasing power and responsibility. And we become competitors with our associates to win promotions. For some, this drive becomes compulsive and emerges as the dominant factor in their lives, even to the exclusion of all else. Competitors have a win/lose philosophy: If I am going to win, then you are going to have to lose. We have all known individuals who, in their frantic effort to get to the top, ruthlessly trample on associates and friends.

The road to the top becomes increasingly narrow. Only a few will make it. Competitors who conclude they will not be able to complete their journey must make a decision.

- They may give up and withdraw from the race.
- They may select a new destination and a new road.
- They can re-evaluate their purpose for life and select new goals.

The duration of this intensive competitive urge varies for each individual. For some it may last from the provider stage to a midlife crisis. Some remain competitive all their lives. Others move on to the advisor stage.

Advisor

The philosophy of the advisor is win/win: If you win, I win. Such individuals opt for the role of a coach rather than that of a "superstar." They concentrate on the task of their group and take pride in the organization's performance. They view their task as consultant, advisor, coordinator, and expediter. They usually motivate by using pleasure rather than pain. Individuals who adopt a win/win philosophy have less difficulty with peer acceptance and their own self-esteem, as opposed to those with a win/lose philosophy. Their value to the organization is enhanced, and they contribute to the welfare of the company by constructive actions rather than by engaging in destructive activities for the purpose of winning.

Many individuals never reach this stage in their life. Others only partially accept this philosophy. For example, they may adopt a win/win attitude for their department but engage in a win/lose relationship with other departments.

Individuals with the win/win philosophy will have a much easier time in making the transition to retirement. Instead of trying to find someone or something to compete with, all they have to do is find someone or some cause to join for expanding their win/win approach.

Reaper

Retirement is the harvest portion of our life. Before farmers can enjoy a harvest, they must sow the seed, till the soil, nurture the crop, and then patiently await its maturity. Only then can they receive the rewards of their past labor. Our early life is the period when we prepare our intellect and plant the seeds (acquired knowledge) for the crop (a self-actualized life) we eventually hope to harvest. Our middle years are spent in nurturing our maturity. Retirement is the harvest.

Retirement is freedom. Freedom, for most, from the expenditure of time to earn money in order to sustain life. Freedom to engage in activities of our choice. Freedom to associate with and be friends with whomever we wish. Freedom to make a contribution to the world if we wish and to do it our own way.

Farmers anticipate the quantity and quality of their harvest by reflecting on the events that preceded the harvest. They know the care they used in preparing the soil and selecting the quality of the seed and they recall the nurture that the crop received in the form of fertilizer, moisture, and sunshine. They watch the crop mature and anticipate and plan the harvest. If they planted wheat, they expect to harvest wheat. Likewise, if they planted corn, corn is what they will harvest.

The harvesting of a lifetime of work is not quite that simple. However, careful and thoughtful reflection on your life to date will give you added insight as to what activities will best assure that you enjoy a zest for life during retirement.

Retirement should be viewed as a continuation of life and an extrapolation of all your prior existence, rather than an abrupt termination of one phase and a totally new beginning to another.

You are not going to have less value as a human being just because you retire. Your perception of yourself may change (as we noted Pete's did, in the last chapter).

You will be essentially the same person, with the same intelligence, skills, talents, abilities, desires, and personality that you were prior to retirement. Your objective is to identify your uniqueness and find ways to use your newly acquired leisure in order to feel you are occupying the summit during your years of retirement.

DISCOVERING THE REAL YOU

Our next effort will be to assist you in additional introspection to better understand your individuality. Be honest with yourself and, to the extent possible, try to avoid either approval or disapproval of past events and feelings. Stand detached as an observer as your self-analysis begins to reveal the real you.

Recalling Your Past

Your first task will be to reflect on your life and recall past joys and occasions when you achieved a sense of accomplishment. Try to concentrate and recall the emotions you experienced as each event occurred. Try to analyze why you think you felt as you did and whether one of Maslow's Needs was involved. After completing your list, place the events in chronological order and identify the stage of life in which the event occurred. Record your work on WS-II.5.1.

Now do the same thing for those occasions that brought dissatisfaction, disappointments, or discontent. This will be more difficult because we tend to forget unpleasant events in our lives. In fact, dredging up past unpleasant situations may be discomforting. But give it a try. Record this information in Section II of the work sheet.

Next, once again review your life and recall earlier goals and fantasies about how you wished to live your life. To the best of your ability, try to determine why you had these goals or dreams. For example, in your early teens you may have wanted to be a doctor. Was it because you wanted to earn a good income, achieve social status, or perhaps because you wanted to ease some of mankind's suffering? Document this information in Section III.

Listing Your Skills and Strengths

Your next task is to make a list of your skills, talents, abilities, and character strengths. If possible, your spouse or a close friend should help you prepare this list. Record this information in Section IV.

Now review all of the material you have recorded on WS II.4.1 and WS-II.5.1 and add or revise as you see fit. Then write your life story, weaving your joys, disappointments, goals, and fantasies into the fabric of your narrative. If possible, relate instances when you used your skills, talents, and other characteristics. Keep the material as brief and concise as possible and yet include all pertinent information. Write and rewrite until you are satisfied that you have captured the real you. Do not be concerned what others may think. After you have a document you are satisfied with, tear it up if you wish. It is important that you be as honest with yourself as possible since this work will become the foundation for the work in the next chapter.

Bill's Story

Let's take a hypothetical individual, Bill, and see how he might go about completing the exercise.

Bill was born in 1918. His family were Midwesterners of moderate means. He remembers 1932 vividly because his father lost his job, and the family faced serious financial problems. In 1934 his father found another job. Bill finished high school in 1936. His parents were supportive of his desire to go to college but had limited resources to help him. He enrolled in a small independent college in the fall of 1936, without any definite idea as to what type of career he wished to pursue. He was leaning toward engineering. In order to finance his education, he worked several jobs a week. A good student, Bill achieved scholastic honors in spite of the time spent on the jobs required to meet his expenses. However, his studies and work left him little time to participate in social activities of the college. Mathematics, economics, and sociology were the subjects which interested him most during his first two years.

During the summer of 1938, he reviewed his career options prior to the mandated declaration of a major in his junior year at the university. After much thought he decided to obtain a teaching certificate. He graduated in June of 1941 and obtained a position teaching mathematics at a medium-sized high school for the 1941-42 school year.

That summer he married Susan, his college sweetheart. She got a job working in a bank.

In December of 1941 the United States entered World War II, and Bill found himself facing induction into the armed services. He applied for, and received, a commission in the Navy and served until 1946. He served as a supply officer with nearly two years of sea duty. Susan continued to work while Bill was in the service.

After his discharge from the Navy, Bill and Susan discussed his career choices. They concluded the financial rewards to be expected from teaching were limited and that he should attempt to find employment with private industry. After several job interviews, he selected a position as a trainee in the corporate office of a large retailing chain. Susan continued to work until 1949, when their first child, a son, was born. After his training period, Bill was assigned to the financial section of his company. He received regular increases and promotions, and he and Susan concluded they had made a good career choice. He liked his work, and they had few financial worries. In 1953 their daughter arrived, and they decided to limit their family to two children.

During the next 12 years Bill had good career progression. He continued to receive salary increases and promotions and in 1958 he became Assistant Vice President in the finance department. In 1962 it seemed as if the bottom had dropped out of Bill's world. Bill's boss received a promotion. An associate (a younger Ivy League MBA) received the boss' job, and Bill would have to report to him. Bill and he had never seen eye to eye, and Bill found reporting to him very difficult. Most of his associates and friends were sympathetic, and Susan did her best to keep his spirits up. However, Bill became more and more depressed. His consumption of alcohol and cigarettes increased. He developed ulcers and high blood pressure. He gained weight.

Bill's friends began to avoid him, and he and Susan began to argue and fight. He considered suicide, quitting his job, leaving his family, and other options. But he did nothing but sink deeper into self-pity. For the first time in his life, Bill truly hated himself.

This situation continued for almost a year until Susan finally persuaded him to seek professional help. The psychologist did help some and convinced Bill he should seek the aid of an executive placement firm. The agency worked with Bill, helped him develop a resume, had him work on his attitude, and gave him some thoughts on the type of firms he might contact for employment. In 1964 Bill obtained a position as V.P. of Finance for a small regional chain of discount stores. The change necessitated moving his family to a new city. His children were very unhappy about changing schools and leaving their friends. His salary was not equal to that of his former position, but with the potential represented by his bonus, stock options, and other perquisites, his total earnings were adequate. He felt much less stress than he had in his former position. He knew he was not going to progress further with his new organization since it was a privately held, family-owned company. Thus he did not have to compete for promotion or practice corporate politics. His relationship with Susan improved. They had an active social life, but their interests became quite divergent. She became active in the League of Women Voters and various civic and philanthropic organizations. He played golf and became active in the local Chamber of Commerce. The children graduated from college, married, and started their careers. Financially he prospered. In 1980, at the age of 62, he realized he must face his mandatory retirement in 1983.

Bill Takes Inventory

Bill began to spend some quiet moments thinking about his interests and how he was going to spend his time after retirement. After unsuccessfully wrestling with the problem for a few weeks, he decided to inventory his skills, talents, and interests. He found difficulty in being objective, wanting instead to credit himself with skills and talents he thought he should have. After a struggle, he compiled the following list:

1. An above-average intelligence, but not brilliant
2. A good knowledge of finance and retailing
3. Communication skills — He could express himself well and organize his thoughts. However, he decided he was not a good listener.
4. Patience — He had acquired this attribute after the trauma of his lost promotion.
5. Intellectual curiosity — He enjoyed acquiring new knowledge.
6. Flexibility — He was willing to change if information or conditions dictated that change was desirable.

He then decided he would carefully review his life and attempt to recall the events that caused him the greatest pleasure and those that gave him the most discomfort. After some time spent on this effort, his list contained the following:

PLEASURE

1. Graduation from college with honors
2. Marriage and his friendship with Susan
3. His teaching position
4. Obtaining his first job after leaving the military
5. His various promotions, especially the Assistant Vice President position early in his career
6. Working with his associates in the discount chain organization

DISCOMFORT
1. His father losing his job during the depression
2. His early college years
3. The missed promotion to Vice President
4. The alienation of wife, family, and friends after the loss of his job

His next step was to go back and try to analyze the significance of the major pleasurable and painful experiences. He tried to relive his emotions as he recalled each event.

Bill was surprised that his early childhood brought forth such strong emotion. He had assumed that his childhood had been normal, with the exception of his father's job loss. The trauma of that event was still vivid in his memory. He could still recall every detail of the night his father returned from work and told them he had lost his job. His mother cried. The look of defeat on his dad's face would always be etched on Bill's memory. His father had aged noticeably while unemployed and never seemed to regain his spirit, even after he got another job. Bill had not really thought about it for years; but now he realized how much of an impact those events had made upon him, and he wondered if those childhood experiences provided the basis for his fierce drive for financial security.

He had also been unhappy in his early college years. His work prevented him from participation in the life of the campus. Several times he had considered quitting school and going to work full-time. He was in college as a student but had few meaningful relationships with other students. His graduation from college with honors proved to him — in his mind — that he was as good as, and maybe even a little better, than most of the other students because he had worked hard for his achievements. He had his ego needs massaged. His teaching year brought fond memories. He could still recall, with a warm feeling, three or four students he had really reached. He believed he had changed their lives for the better. During that period, for the first time in his life, he had experienced a sense of self-fulfillment.

As he recalled his courtship and marriage to Susan, he was flooded with warm memories. They had been very much in love. Sure, sex had been a part of it, but more important, for the first time in his life, he had another human being with whom he could share his innermost thoughts. They spent long hours talking and getting to know each other better. He sincerely regretted not having that sort of relationship with her today.

And then his war years. But it hadn't been all bad. The separation from Susan had been difficult, and the combat experience had been frightening. It seemed the war would never end. But for the first time he had developed genuine friendships with some of his shipmates. As he looked back, he realized he had never had any true friends in his childhood. He really didn't have anyone who could be classified as a close friend today. He recognized the need to attempt to develop his ability to make and retain friends.

He recalled the occasion when he had been accepted as a trainee by the retail chain. He had told Susan he was on his way and had described how he would work hard, progress, and provide her and the children's every need and want. And he had worked hard. Every moment was dedicated to thinking and planning on how he was going to reach that next rung in the ladder.

And somewhere in that frantic scramble, the children were born. Looking at his list he suddenly realized that their birth was not listed among his most joyous moments. He had been so preoccupied with the job that he had not functioned as a parent. And they had grown up without his actually knowing them. Perhaps retirement would afford him the opportunity to become better acquainted with them. And he could spend a lot of time with his grandchildren. He also began to understand for the first time that it had been at that point in his life that Susan and his relationship had begun to deteriorate. She had the full responsibility of raising the children and probably resented his failure to help and spend time with them. As the relationship had cooled, he turned more to his work and she to the job of raising the children. She had become active in PTA, scouts, and similar groups.

As he had turned to his work, he increasingly savored the recognition he received from the company. The various promotions and increased responsibilities brought much needed ego gratification. But nothing had equaled his promotion to Assistant Vice President. That was "proof positive" that he was a fast-track individual, and he was only 40. He felt self-confident and, yes, even superior.

Looking back he realized that he had changed at that time. He became somewhat arrogant, demanding of his subordinates, and contemptuous of others' weaknesses. He was going to get to the top no matter who might be in the way. Now, he would have to admit, he had become a person whom he would not want as a friend. His ego needs at that time did not allow room for friendships.

And then unexpectedly he received one of the greatest shocks of his life. He could still recall it as vividly as if it had happened yesterday. His boss called him into his office, and he knew that it was to tell him he was getting his job. The grapevine had it that the boss was being promoted. He and his associates had discussed it, and they had told him he was the logical candidate. After all, he had more experience, more knowledge, more of everything than his competitors.

After a few moments of small talk, his boss had said, "Bill, as you probably have heard, I am being promoted. Harry is taking my job. I am sure you will give him the same help and support that you have given me." He was stunned. He thought, this has to be a joke. I must have heard him wrong. His head buzzed. He cannot now recall what he had said. He can remember he got up and left the office and went to a bar, even though it was only two o'clock in the afternoon. He sat there dazed, his thoughts flitting between fighting the decision (by appealing to the president of the company) to quitting. His confidence was completely shattered. His self-esteem gone.

The next few months had been like a nightmare. His actions were irrational. If Susan hadn't finally convinced him he needed professional help, he would have become an alcoholic. But he did get help, regrouped, and started again.

Looking back, he could now concede maybe it was for the best. His new job provided him with an opportunity to assist his new company. They needed his experience and knowledge. It was a team effort to improve their performance. It wasn't a personal struggle to be recognized and promoted. It was a feeling of "us against the world" rather than "me against you." Sure there were still times of stress, but of a different type. He hadn't that "tightly wound feeling" he had before.

His relationship with the family had improved. He did wish that he and Susan could recapture some of their old relationship, but she had her own interests now. And now he was facing retirement in a couple of years. He didn't feel that old. Still, he was looking forward to more leisure time. He realized that he was going to have to do something that would give him a sense that there was still a purpose for his life. What? He didn't know, but at least he understood himself a little better.

I think Bill did a good job of self-analysis. He still has much work to do in developing a plan to assure that his retirement activities give his life a sense of purpose.

The next chapter concerns our needs in retirement and methods for making choices to assure a successful retirement.

Chapter 6
Why am I?

Why am I?

Retirement is a gift of time — probably some 175,000 hours of time. Our sense of well-being in retirement depends largely upon how we choose to use this time. Used properly, it can lead to a fervor and a zest for life. Improperly used, time can lead to boredom and lethargy. A balanced use of your retirement time will provide the best possibility that your life will have meaning. We will explore the use of time to satisfy intellectual, physical, and spiritual needs.

INTELLECTUAL STIMULATION

One of the myths about aging is that as we grow older our capacity to learn is impaired. This has been disproved. Most authorities agree that there is no significant decline in intelligence as we grow older. Unless we are limited by emotional or physical factors, we retain the capacity to learn. For life to continue to have meaning, we should continue to use our intellectual capacity. "Use it or lose it" is as applicable to our mental capacity as it is to our muscular vigor. All too frequently you hear retirees make a statement such as "After a year of retirement I felt like my mind had turned to mush." Careful questioning will often reveal that the individual went from an environment of vigorous intellectual activity in their preretirement years to a postretirement life style completely lacking in mental stimulation. The selection of the appropriate intellectual stimulation is an individual matter and should be tailored to personal interests, talents, and background. The following suggestions are by no means a complete or all-inclusive list of possibilities.

Systematic Pursuit of Knowledge

Many retired individuals use a portion of their newly acquired time to enroll in various types of educational programs. Others choose a program of self-study. Some may wish to acquire knowledge to increase their enjoyment of some planned interest or activity. An example would be the study of a language or history to increase the enjoyment of future travel. Others pursue new knowledge simply for the joy of intellectual stimulation.

Advisory and/or Teaching Activities

In other cultures and in times past in our country, the elderly continued to a part of the family and were valued for their advice and counsel. Their knowledge was respected, and their lives had meaning.

Such a relationship is rare in our culture, but an alternative is possible. Consulting, teaching, and other advisory roles provide an opportunity for a retiree to share a lifetime of acquired knowledge and skills with others. The role of consultant can be compensated or volunteered. Opportunities exist to serve as a member of the board of directors or on advisory boards of for-profit or nonprofit organizations. One can become associated with an established group of consultants or form one's own consulting service. Many opportunities for teaching exist. Junior colleges often provide opportunities for retirees to share their knowledge with others, either on a regular or part-time basis. Church groups, social agencies, and philanthropic groups have the need for individuals who have time to volunteer their services. The possibilities are limited only by the limits of your imagination. A resourceful individual can create opportunities to serve that will be tailored to his or her unique talents and experience.

Hobbies and Crafts

Many retirees obtain deep satisfaction from hobbies and crafts. The acquisition of the required knowledge and the creation of an item of beauty or utility gives a sense of accomplishment. Woodworking, painting, sculpting, writing, music, gardening, and collecting are but a few of the many opportunities. Many times the hobby or craft can be a source of income. Even though you may not need the additional funds, the proof of the value of your efforts, demonstrated by the fact that someone is willing to pay you for your product, may add to your satisfaction. The selection of a hobby or craft that stimulates your intellectual, creative, and aesthetic needs can add immeasurably to your zest for living.

Intellectual Games

Intellectual stimulation can be achieved by the improvement of the playing skills associated with intellectual games. The ability to play a good game of bridge, chess, or backgammon can be stimulating and enjoyable. The resultant interpersonal relationships also assist in fulfilling social needs.

Political Activity

The future welfare of our communities, states, and the nation is largely dependent upon our political system. And the individuals who are elected, and their actions shape our destiny. Because of the increasing complexities of our society, it is easy to become cynical about politics and adopt the attitude that it is useless for an individual to attempt to change the system. By so doing, however, we allow the future of our children and grandchildren to be decided by self-interest and special-interest groups. As a retiree, age and experience have given you insights that are badly needed by society. To withhold these skills and knowledge from the political process is to short change our nation's future. Most of us, as we grow older, become aware that there are few absolutes of right or wrong. Most decisions deal in shades of gray. Only after carefully weighing all facets of a problem can we hope to come up with the best solution. Retirement gives us the time and the knowledge necessary to study the complexities of an issue. If you decide that involvement in politics would interest you, you should make a choice as to how you can best serve. You may wish simply to improve your knowledge of the candidates and issues so you can be a more informed and competent elector. You might choose to work for the political party of your choice or for a political candidate. Some may choose to become well informed about a particular national problem, such as hazardous waste, and become an advocate, even if only by influencing family or friends on the issue. You could run for an elective office such as the school board or city council. The opportunities are many. The main thing is to become concerned and informed and involve yourself where your interests and talents can make the most contribution.

Traveling

Most people enjoy traveling. Some may restrict their excursions to this continent, while others may choose international junkets. If, in addition to enjoying the sights and scenery, one uses the opportunity to learn about the history, culture, and customs of the places visited, the enjoyment of the trip can be greatly enhanced.

Investments

The financial decisions required of retirees will influence whether they continue to enjoy financial security. Making prudent investments (balancing the dollar risk and the purchasing power reward) become more imperative with a fixed income. The acquisition and enhancement of investment knowledge provides intellectual stimulation and may contribute to your financial security. There are a number of ways to achieve the increased knowledge. College courses, seminars, periodicals, books, and television programs are but a few of the many avenues to learning you may wish to pursue.

A Second or Continued Career

Many individuals choose a part-time or full-time job after retirement. There is a growing trend for companies to allow employees to serve as part-time workers or consultants after retirement. If additional income is not required, the retiree should determine the extent to which the consulting service will be valued and used. If the arrangement is motivated primarily by social concerns rather than the belief the retiree's continued service will be of value, it may lead to disillusionment and disappointment. Other retirees elect to start a small business. Again, unless a retiree's finances require the additional income, care should be taken to assure that the time spent on the business will be enjoyable and stimulating. It should not be undertaken simply to avoid boredom.

This list of sources of intellectual stimulation is by no means complete. It should be used by preretirees to stimulate their thinking about the various options available to continue their intellectual stimulation.

SPIRITUAL STIMULATION

Webster defines spirit as "the feeling part of man as distinguished from the body." In discussing our spiritual needs in this material, we are referring to that element in humans that seeks relationships with others. To have a meaningful relationship there must be a giving and receiving on the part of both parties. Individuals vary greatly in their capacity to relate to others. Let's assume that we can measure an individual's spiritual development on a scale of

1 to 10. On the 1 end of the scale we would place the person who is interested only in himself or herself and who uses others to further personal needs and desires. On the 10 side we would place the individual who is primarily interested in the needs of others and who has only minimal concerns for his or her personal welfare. Spiritual maturity can be considered the process of moving from the lower end of the scale to the higher end. A few self-centered individuals are only concerned with their own welfare and do not establish meaningful relationships with anyone, not even their spouse and family. Also a few have a genuine concern for mankind as a whole and give of themselves and assets freely, without thoughts of recognition or rewards for their efforts. Most of us fall somewhere on the middle portion of the chart.

Theology, psychiatry, medicine, and sociology all suggest that our sense of well-being is improved if we function somewhere above the lower end of the scale.

Let's assume a 5 rating would be given to individuals who have meaningful relationships with their spouse, children, and two or three close friends. If these individuals wished to further their spiritual development, they could plan to upgrade some of their acquaintances to close friends and/or become concerned and active in promoting the welfare of some particular work or cause.

An example might be a concern for the apparent increase in the number of battered and abused children and enrollment in a program dedicated to determining the causes and prevention of this evil. If one has religious beliefs, retirement will afford the opportunity to become more involved in church activities.

The gift of time offered by retirement gives us a golden opportunity to increase our spiritual maturity. Both preretirees and retirees should determine their spiritual maturity. If they elect to improve their spiritual development, they should adopt a program that will assist them in fulfilling their spiritual needs.

We will deal with the subject further under the section on Wellness (Section III). At this time, reflect on your spiritual maturity and assign yourself a rating. Record your rating on WS-II.6.1.

PHYSICAL NEEDS

A healthy and well-conditioned body adds to our sense of well being. Retirement offers many opportunities to improve the tone and functioning of the body. The opportunity for enjoyable exercise is increased. You will have more time for golf, tennis, hiking, or bicycling. Yard work and gardening provide opportunities to exercise. Many hobbies such as woodworking and gem collecting also provide opportunities for physical exercise. Dancing and swimming are also excellent forms of exercise. One can always elect to engage in an exercise program, either at home or at a gymnasium. Whatever your selection, the chances of your continuing your program will be improved if you select those activities that give you enjoyment. Retirement plans should include activities that will promote your physical fitness.

RECREATION

Many people look forward to their retirement with the thought that it will provide them with time for their favorite forms of recreation. They find it hard to believe that they should still plan to take vacations. Webster defines recreation as "refreshment of body and mind." Even a life totally devoted to fun and games requires periods of change and refreshment. While it is certainly proper that your retirement life style should include those activities that give you pleasure and satisfaction, it is also true that your satisfaction will be dulled if you do not plan for periods of time involving activities that refresh and recreate the vitality of your emotional being. It is important that you continue to take vacations and other periodic respites from your retirement activities.

Revisiting Bill

We are now going to watch Bill as he continues his planning process to assure that his retirement activities give his life a sense of purpose.

As Bill rethinks his past, he realizes that the Depression and his father's losing his job have instilled in him a strong need for financial security. Reviewing his financial resources, he concludes he will have ample income and assets to enable him and Susan to satisfy their needs and wants during retirement.

Next, Bill looks at his interpersonal relationships. He concludes that he would like to improve his relationship with his family, and especially with Susan. Most of his acquaintances are business associates, and he has no one he can classify as a close friend. He recognizes this is an area where he needs to do some work. He evaluates himself on the spiritual maturity scale and classifies himself as a 3. He determines he would like to strive for at least a 5 rating.

Why am I? 165

He next evaluates his self-esteem. He concludes that basically he likes himself. Retirement will give him an opportunity to make some friends in order to enhance his support system, so he does not anticipate any problems with self-esteem.

Bill concludes that unless he takes some positive action, he may have significant problems with his need to have a purpose for his life in retirement. He realizes he must do something now and not leave that area of his life to chance. He begins to develop a plan. He once again reviews his life and recalls those events that brought him the greatest satisfaction. He decides that having friends and serving as a teacher and advisor to others should be a part of his retirement life style.

He realizes that just wishing for something is not going to cause it to happen. If it were a business problem, he would use the principles of planning. The first task would be to decide on a strategic plan — that is, what is the general direction the business would take to accomplish its mission? The strategic plan he must develop is to determine how to use the time he will have in retirement to assure he has a purpose for life. But one of the principles of business planning involves getting as many people as practical involved in the planning process. He and Susan are going to share the retirement, so he should involve her in the project.

He discusses with Susan his impending retirement and the conclusions he has reached to date. He is delighted to find she also wants to improve their relationship.

Deciding they should collectively look at their interests, they prepare the following list:

INTERESTS	SUSAN	BILL
Golf	L	M
Bridge	H	L
Travel	M	M
Dancing	M	L
Investments	L	H
Art	H	L
Reading	H	H
Horticulture	H	L
H = High Interest	M = Medium Interest	L = Low Interest

The following summarizes their discussions:

Golf They decided they should keep the membership in the country club after retirement. Bill had been playing on Saturday, with an occasional weekday game with a client or business associate. Bill concludes he would enjoy playing more golf, and they agree that a membership in the club and more active participation will provide them with a good opportunity to meet new people. Susan decides she will take golf instruction from the pro and begin playing on Tuesdays with the ladies' group.

Bridge They presently play an occasional game of social bridge. Susan belongs to a women's bridge group and is a much better player than Bill. They decide to increase the frequency of play and to explore the possibility of receiving bridge instructions at a continuing education course sponsored by the local junior college. They conclude that this activity will also give them an opportunity to meet new couples and make new acquaintances.

Travel Both enjoy travel. However their vacations have been restricted to a two-week period because Bill feels that is the maximum amount of time he should be away from the company. They agree they would enjoy more leisurely travel and that study of prospective travel options would increase their appreciation of the locations visited. If they had even a limited ability to communicate with the people of some of the foreign countries they would like to visit, it would improve their enjoyment of their travels. They will explore the possibilities of learning conversational Spanish.

Dancing Bill is surprised to learn that Susan thoroughly enjoys dancing. He has never taken any dancing lessons and feels inadequate, especially when dancing with someone other than Susan. They decide to take dancing lessons and participate more in the dances held at the country club.

Investments Bill has handled all the financial matters of the family. Their discussion reveals that Susan has resented this. She would like to know more about their financial situation and investments. They decide to attend some financial seminars together. Bill agrees he will inform Susan as to their existing financial resources and that they will jointly evaluate and concur upon any future changes in their investment portfolio.

Art Susan has studied art and enjoys visiting art galleries and art showings. Bill knows nothing about the subject but would like to learn. Susan will recommend some books on the subject. They will go to local art galleries, and she will help him gain an appreciation for art. They also will plan to include art galleries in their future travel plans.

Reading Susan enjoys reading. She spends several hours a week reading current best sellers as well as old masterpieces of literature. Bill also reads extensively, but his reading has been confined to articles, periodicals, and books that pertain to his profession and business. Bill decides he would enjoy recreational reading, and they look forward to reading some of the same books and discussing them afterwards.

Horticulture They have used a landscape maintenance service for the past several years. Bill had enjoyed yard work until the demands of the job became so great that he began to resent the time required to take care of the lawn and shrubbery. He decided he would enjoy yard work once again after retirement, when he would have sufficient time for the required maintenance. Susan reveals that she envies those that raise orchids and always wanted a greenhouse. They have an ideal location for a greenhouse and agree to explore the feasibility of having one built.

These discussions covered several evenings, and both agree that they feel much closer than they have for several years. They are looking forward to Bill's retirement.

Bill is pleased that he decided to include Susan in the strategic portion of their retirement planning. He recalls that another part of the process of strategic planning is to determine if there are sufficient resources to carry out the plan. Since he has already determined they have the financial resources, the remaining resource required is time. He does not want his retirement life style to be so programed that he will feel pressured by the constraints of time. Conversely he does not want so much spare time on his hands that he will be bored. He therefore decides to analyze how he is now spending his time. The following is the result of his analysis:

TYPICAL WEEK'S ACTIVITIES
Present Average Use of Time

	Hrs.	%
Maintenance Activities:		
Sleeping, Personal Grooming, etc.	56	
Meals	14	
Reading Newspaper, TV News, etc.	5	
Exercise Program, Walking, Calisthenics, etc.	5	
Sub Total	80	48%
Job-Related Activities:		
Working and Commuting	50	
After-Hours Reading, Reports, Trade Journals, etc.	10	
Job-Related Socializing	4	
Sub Total	64	38%
Recreation and Miscellaneous Activities:		
Golf	6	
Watching TV (Recreational)	4	
Socializing	4	
Miscellaneous	10	
Sub Total	24	14%
Total Week	168	100%

Bill decides that after retirement the time spent on the items he has classified as maintenance activities will not change. He next looked at the retirement activities he and Susan had planned for their retirement. He decided that consulting might also be an area of interest and prepared a time-allocation chart as shown below:

TYPICAL WEEK'S ACTIVITIES
Average Use of Time in Retirement

	Hrs.	%
Maintenance Activities	80	48%
Intellectual Stimulation		
Consulting	20	
Reading, Study and Courses	10	
Handling of Personal Finances	4	
Sub Total	34	20%
Physical Stimulation		
Gardening	6	
Golf (Time on the Course)	12	
Dancing (Time on the Floor)	1	
Sub Total	19	11%

Spiritual Stimulation
- Golf (Socializing After the Game) — 3
- Dancing (Socializing) — 3
- Bridge — 3
- Time with Children and Grandchildren — 6
- Political Activity — 4
- Sub Total — 19 — 11%
- Discretionary Time — 16 — 10%
- Total Week — 168 — 100%

Looking over his table and the time allotted to each category, Bill was satisfied with the result. He felt his activities would be stimulating, and yet he had allowed himself enough discretionary time so that his life style would be relaxed. He approves of the balance between the time spent on intellectual, physical, and spiritual needs.

He is satisfied with the strategic plan. His next task, he realizes, is to develop tactical and operational plans. The activity that will require the most thought and effort will be the plan to engage in consulting work after his retirement. He decides the tactical plan for consulting should specify how he proposes to carry out this activity, and the operational plan should include specifics, such as identifying subtasks and establishing a time schedule for completion. The following is the way he went about building these plans.

Bill first determined just what consultant, advisory, or teaching role he wished to pursue after retirement. He gave the matter considerable thought and concluded that there was a need for consultants in the retail business. He was familiar with their problems and operations since he had spent a lifetime in the retail business. He had a long association with many owners of this type of business. He began to identify their needs and the knowledge and skills he possessed that would make it possible for him to make a worthwhile contribution with his consulting service. He decided they needed help in the following areas:
- Budgeting
- Inventory Control
- Cost Analysis
- Finance
- Data Processing

He knew how each of the above, with the exception of data processing, was handled by his organization. He would have to analyze how the procedures should be modified to fit the needs of the small retailer. He had several bright young men on his staff who had handled the introduction of data processing to his organization. The introduction of smaller and more efficient computers into the marketplace undoubtedly meant they had application to the small independent retail establishment. He would have to become better informed on data processing.

He concluded that his next step should be to develop a marketing plan. He would have to determine the best method of selecting and contacting potential clients, the sales presentation and closing, and the method of charging the client. He recalled that he had several acquaintances who did consulting for his company and that they would be a good resource for information to help him get started. As for the fees, he would keep them modest. His finances were such that he did not need the money. He would take any profit he made and set up a trust for his grandchildren's eduction. That would relieve his children of that financial responsibility and assure his grandchildren of an excellent base from which to get their start in the world.

He had a couple of years until retirement; and if he worked and developed his plan, he should be ready to start his consulting business shortly after retiring.

He would also develop tactical and operational plans for the other retirement activities. The requirement for detail would vary with each.

It is impossible and improper for any of us to judge the merits of Bill's plan. Just as we cannot tell a youth that he or she should become a doctor or an engineer, we cannot judge what a retiree's interests and activities should be. Each plan depends upon the retiree's abilities, interests, and skills. Each should tailor activities to fit his or her uniqueness. If after Bill retires he awakens each morning with excitement and eagerness for the new day and experiences a zest for life, then his plan is a success. If not, he should do more work and more planning. Each of us should realize that retirement is an opportunity to live at the summit of our life. We should not settle for less.

I suggest you complete the work on your strategic plan for retirement by completing WS-II.6.1.

After that you will be ready to move on to your tactical and operational plans. The suggested procedure is covered in the next chapter.

Chapter 7
How?

How?

There is no clear delineation of the boundaries between strategic, tactical, and operational planning. And it is not important that you try to establish such a division. It is important that you complete your planning.

STRATEGIC PLANNING

Perhaps if we discuss an instance that requires a very simple plan, we can better understand the process.

Let's say you decide you wish to travel to Europe. That is your strategy. Next you decide to spend two weeks in England and to get there by airplane. Those are tactics. The purchase of the ticket, selection of an itinerary, and arranging for hotel reservations are related to operational planning. You will note that we start with a very general and broad goal and then become more specific, and finally identify the individual tasks necessary to make your plan operational.

Often the failure to follow a strategic plan with the necessary tactical and operational plans results in the failure to carry out the desired activity. For example, the individual who at 55 decides he would like to learn a foreign language, but does not follow up with additional planning, will be saying at 60, 65, 70, and 75, "I want to learn a foreign language." At his funeral someone may say, "He was a nice guy. He wanted to learn a foreign language." His problem was that he did not decide which language he would study or how he would obtain the necessary knowledge. He might have selected a tape, textbooks, a Berlitz-type course, or a course at a junior college. He also needed to decide when he would commence. He lacked tactical and operational plans.

You will recall that Bill decided he would like to spend a part of his time after retirement in an advisory, teaching, or consulting role. That is strategy. He narrowed this down to a plan for part-time consulting. That is tactics. He then began identifying subtasks:

the type of consulting activity, marketing plan, and fee structure. That is the beginning of operational planning. He needs to be more specific about how and when to have a workable operational plan.

TACTICAL PLANNING

In many instances there are a number of tactics you can use to accomplish a strategy. Bill, for example, could elect to teach part-time rather than consult. Or he could elect to join an existing consulting group rather than start his own business. If you find your tactics are limited, perhaps you should go back and attempt to broaden your strategy. Give yourself as many options as possible for arriving at where you want to go.

Your next task is to evaluate the tactical options. You may wish to start by listing the positive and negative factors you perceive for each tactic. This list may give you some clear indication as to the best alternative for you. After you have narrowed your choices to one or two, use your imagination to evaluate your potential satisfaction with your selections. Find a quiet place where you can relax and concentrate. Imagine you are engaged in the activities of your choice. Think of some of the positive factors on your list. How do you feel? Select some of the negative possibilities. Evaluate your emotions. You have many years of experience that should be helpful in improving the quality of your decisions.

If you decide that you wish to start implementing your tactical choice, move on to operational planning. If you decide to discard a tactical choice, select another for testing in the above manner. Or perhaps you need to go back and reevaluate your strategy.

The amount of time and effort you should spend on evaluating your tactical options is dependent upon the magnitude of your commitment of resources and the significance of the tactic.

For example, Bill's decision to do part-time consulting work will necessitate a substantial commitment of time and effort in preparation prior to his actual consulting activities. He should do everything possible to assure it is an activity that will fulfill his expectations.

Likewise, if one of the activities is to play golf and this necessitates joining an expensive country club, one should be assured that golf is an activity he would enjoy before making a sizeable expenditure for a country club membership.

The decision to spend a part of your time in recreational reading would not require or warrant extensive planning effort.

OPERATIONAL PLANNING

A selected tactical plan should be followed by operational planning. All of the necessary tasks should be identified and decisions made about how and when they will be completed.

The process should be repeated for each tactical plan as appropriate.

You are probably asking: "Just how long before I retire should I get active in my planning?"

I would suggest that at some time around age 50 to 55 you should begin to develop your strategic plan (your planned retirement activities). Perhaps some five years before retirement you should develop the tactical plans, followed by the operational plans. Within two or three years of retirement, you should have completed your planning activities.

Recently a survey of a large group of retirees asked "If you had it to do over, what would you do differently?" The number one answer was "I would start my planning for retirement much earlier."

Perhaps some readers of this book are already retired. Is it too late for you? Definitely not. If you desire more zest in your life, go through the entire planning process and see if you can identify and create activities that will bring new meaning to your life.

It is desireable that you have an inventory of potential activities available. For example, the onset of arthritis might prevent your participation in golf, and you would need some other activity to substitute for the time spent at golf. Alternative and contingency planning are as important for designing a life with a purpose as it was for planning for financial independence.

I would suggest you document your planning and include the information with the work sheets you have and will be developing.

The procedures suggested in this action are just that, suggestions. There is no intent to infer that this is the only method or even the best method. Each of you should adopt, delete, or modify any material as you see fit. The important thing is not the process. The important thing is to develop a life style during your retirement years that will bring you happiness and a zest for life.

The goal for you is to awake each morning feeling:

THE BEST IS YET TO BE!

SECTION III:
Wellness

Chapter 1—What is Wellness?......................179
Chapter 2—Physical Health..........................185
Chapter 3—Emotional Health......................195
Chapter 4—Spiritual Health........................211
Chapter 5—Your Plan for Wellness................219

Chapter 1

What is Wellness?

What is Wellness?

In order to feel vigorous, vital, and self-fulfilled we must cultivate and maintain a state of wellness. A machine needs all of its parts to perform effectively the task for which it was designed. A human being needs good physical fitness, emotional health, and spiritual maturity in order to function properly.

ACHIEVING A BALANCE

Unfortunately, most of us spend more time and effort on the care and maintenance of our automobile than we do on our state of wellness.

Some individuals concentrate their attention and efforts on only a portion of their being. They may concentrate on physical fitness and ignore their emotional and spiritual needs. This makes about as much sense as providing excellent maintenance to your automobile's engine but ignoring the transmission and brakes. If you neglect the proper care of a machine, you can always discard it and purchase another. You are not offered that option with your life. You have only one opportunity; there is no second chance.

Many abuse their physical bodies, allow their mental processes to become contaminated, and ignore their spiritual needs. They erroneously believe they can delay maintenance and development until some later date when conditions will be more advantageous. We recognize that the engine of our car must be serviced and maintained, or it will ultimately fail. We cannot allow it to operate over an extended period of time without lubrication and then expect to make up for our past neglect by resuming proper maintenance procedures. Neither can we abuse our health without paying a price.

DEGREE OF WELLNESS

Health is not just not being sick. Health is functioning at, or near, our potential. There are degrees of wellness just as there are degrees of sickness. The following chart illustrates this point.

THE QUALITY OF LIFE

HEALTH ⟶ WELLNESS

PHYSICAL	EMOTIONAL	SPIRITUAL
Healthy Good physical condition and alert mental state	Healthy Well-integrated emotionally and generally happy	Healthy Feeling in control of your life Progressing toward the achievement of your ultimate concern
Health Problems High blood pressure Diabetes Angina attacks Arthritis, etc.	Mildly Neurotic Pessimistic Experiencing attacks of anxiety and/or depression	Adequate Self-Esteem
Disability Stroke Severe heart trouble Emphysema, etc.	Severe Neurosis Psychotic	Egotistical Self Centered
Early Death	Inability to cope Needs custodial care	Narcissistic

ILLNESS

It is possible for individuals to have excellent physical health and at the same time suffer from depression and lack of self-esteem. Their failure to obtain high levels of emotional and spiritual health, however, detracts from their state of wellness. Your goal should be to achieve good physical health, a positive mental outlook, and self-actualization.

Failure to attain emotional health may lead to physical problems. For example, prolonged periods of excessive stress often results in physical health problems. Likewise the failure to attain spiritual maturity may result in a failure to optimize emotional health. The individual who fails to develop self-esteem is unlikely to develop a zest for life.

If you are to achieve a high degree of wellness, you must devote time and effort to developing and maintaining physical, emotional, and spiritual health. And your efforts must be coordinated, due to the interaction of each upon the others.

TAKING TIME TO SMELL THE ROSES

Poets and philosophers frequently point out that life is a journey. It seems to me that too often we are overly concerned with how fast we are traveling and give insufficient attention to the quality of the voyage. We live our lives in the same manner that some people take long automobile trips. We drive at high speeds for long hours. We focus our attention on the narrow ribbon of concrete before us and fail to enjoy the experience of traveling. Never pausing at a scenic site to be refreshed, we become too tired and tense to enjoy the trip. We take pride in the distances covered and lose sight of the purpose for the travel. Many fail to provide the proper maintenance for their vehicle and experience a break down before the journey is completed.

In life we have only one opportunity to experience and enjoy the passing environment. Our failure to fully experience each moment of our existence is an opportunity lost forever.

From what I have said so far, you may conclude that I am an advocate of a life spent in self-gratification. Nothing could be further from the truth. A successful journey through life requires planning and includes experiencing pain, self-denial, and introspection. We must understand our total being and know what it means to be human. In other words we need to have insight into what contributes to our wellness.

In the next chapter we will discuss physical health. Chapter 3 will cover emotional health, and Chapter 4 deals with spiritual maturity.

Chapter 2

Physical Health

Physical Health

The vehicle we use to convey ourselves through life is our physical body and intellect. The end of the journey is death. Most of us hope to delay experiencing the end of the journey as long as possible — that is, providing our health is sufficiently good in our later years to enable us to continue to enjoy living.

INCREASED LIFE EXPECTANCY

Modern medicine has greatly increased our chances of reaching our alloted years of four-score and ten. At the turn of this century, life expectancy in the United States was 47 years. Today you can expect that your physical body will serve you into your seventh decade. The greatest contributor to a longer life has been the discovery of various antibiotics and vaccines. Death from tuberculosis, polio, pneumonia, influenza, malaria, typhoid, and other infectious diseases has been dramatically reduced, if not entirely eliminated. In 1920 infectious diseases were twice as apt to be the cause of death as all other causes combined. Today, heart diseases and strokes contribute to over one-half of the deaths in the United States. This is true in spite of the introduction of coronary by-pass surgery, heart valve implants, pacemakers, and other new marvels of medicine that can repair a damaged cardiovascular system.

The human body gradually wears out. The deterioration we experience is due to degenerative diseases. Heart attacks, strokes, and arthritis are examples of impairments we suffer that are brought about by the deterioration of our bodies. Since, as we have noted, degenerative diseases of the cardiovascular system (our heart and blood vessels) are the leading causes of death today, if we could find some way of slowing the damage to this system, we could greatly extend the life expectancy of our population and improve the quality of life in our later years.

Most of us are born with a healthy heart and blood vessels. Early in life we start destroying that system. The type of fuel we use to propel our machine corrodes our fuel lines, and our sedentary life style fails to provide our fuel pump with the exercises it needs to remain healthy. We have the knowledge necessary to dramatically reduce the number of deaths caused by the deterioration of our cardiovascular system. But we cannot rely on the medical profession alone to repair our damaged system. We must each establish our own health plan if we hope to increase the probability that we will live our alloted years and have good physical health during the later part of our journey.

CARDIOVASCULAR FUNCTIONS

At this point let's take a brief look at how the cardiovascular system functions. Our blood vessels (arteries, capillaries, and veins) can be thought of as our body's fuel system. They carry nutrients to the millions of cells that make up our physical body. Much of the garbage that our body produces is also transported through this conduit to our sewage disposal units (our kidneys and lungs). Our heart is the pump that causes this life-sustaining movement through our circulatory system.

We can predict that a restriction in the traffic-carrying capacity of our circulatory system or a deterioration in the efficiency of our pump will lead to a decline in health. Our physical body is an assemblage of many and varied cells. Any decline in our ability to adequately nurture these basic building blocks of our body will lead to a decline in their efficiency and thus our general health. Likewise, if the removal of wastes from these units is hindered, we can become poisoned from our own waste products.

Medical science is proving that this is just what is happening. The problem is not primarily one of aging. The causative factor is the way we choose to live — the food we eat and the amount and type of our physical activity. Our diet creates blockages in our circulatory system, and our physical inactivity allows our heart to become inefficient.

CARDIOVASCULAR DEGENERATION

It may seem strange that, despite all the wonders of modern technology, we are only now acquiring the knowledge necessary to make specific recommendations as to how to prevent the many unnecessary deaths caused by premature degeneration of our cardiovascular system. However, there are several reasons why it has only been recently that the general public has become aware of the facts behind cardiovascular deterioration.

As has been discussed, during the first part of this century the major cause of death was infectious diseases. Medical science's thinking was heavily oriented to identifying the cause and cure for those types of illnesses. Degenerative diseases become obvious only in an older population since the deterioration is gradual, and health is impaired only when the damage has progressed over an extended period of time. Thus with the increase in life expectancy, we are becoming more aware of the true magnitude of the problem of degenerative diseases.

An infectious disease is caused by the invasion of some foreign organism into our bodies. Medical science has been very successful in identifying the invaders and devising treatments to assist our bodies in repelling the attack. Degenerative disease is a deterioration of the effective functioning of our bodies, and it is difficult to identify the existence and cause of the premature decline in the effectiveness of our internal organs. In fact, in most cases, it is only after autopsies are performed on the deceased, that an exact determination can be made as to the degree of the degeneration.

Since the degeneration of our cardiovascular system is gradual (and the possible causes are many and varied), it takes extensive research to identify the causative factors. The chemical composition of our food, the amount and type of our physical exercise, our emotional state, the environment, and the normal aging process are all possible contributors to the deterioration. With so many contributors and the length of time required to validate controlled studies, the difficulty of obtaining scientific proof as to the causes of degenerative disease is understandable.

The medical profession receives its greatest economic rewards by treating illnesses. Our society has not chosen to allocate a significant portion of its health dollar to pure research on methods of promoting wellness.

As long as the deterioration is not severe enough to cause personal health problems, we somehow believe we are immune from degenerative diseases. We resist making fundamental changes in our basic life style. And, we resist facing the truth that we alone have the primary responsibility for maintaining the efficiency of our body.

So, while there are any number of excuses for failure to give the proper attention to the causes of cardiovascular failure, we can no longer pass the buck. Our knowledge has progressed to the point that we can pinpoint what needs to be done to improve our cardiovascular health.

Placque in the Arteries

One problem is the buildup of plaque in our arteries. This buildup is gradual. As the process continues, it narrows (or even eventually blocks) the blood vessels, hindering their ability to provide nutrients to the many cells of our body. In some instances a portion of the plaque breaks away from the location where it was formed. The plaque then travels through the system of blood vessels until it lodges, and thus obstructs the flow of blood. Downstream, the cells are starved and die. When this occurs in the blood vessels of the brain, the individual experiences a stroke. If the blockage starves the muscles of the heart, a heart attack occurs. The plaque formation on the walls of the arteries leads to the formation of a fibrous substance in the walls of the arteries. This limits the elasticity of the walls, and we experience something called "hardening of the arteries." This is a contributor, in many instances, to high blood pressure.

The process of the buildup of plaque and the scarring of the walls of the arteries is slow but cumulative, so its damage to health usually becomes evident only in our later years. The fact that it is happening is irrefutable. The question that medical science has been wrestling with for the past two or three decades is, Is the buildup of plaque in our arteries a normal part of aging? The answer is no — at least not to the extent we are experiencing it in the United States population.

In many cultures, the instances of cardiovascular disease among the older population is very low. This led to studies to determine differences between their life styles and ours. One of the obvious differences was the amount of fat in the diets of the different cultures. Our typical diet consists of over 40 percent fat. The diet of countries with low instances of cardiovascular diseases was much lower, often 10 percent or less.

If diet is the problem, then the beginning of the disease should be evidenced in our younger population. In the Korean and Vietnam wars, hundreds of autopsies were performed on our soldiers killed in battle. More than half were found to have damage to their arteries caused by the buildup of plaque. Japan made studies of the arteries of many of their young who died in accidents and found that artery damage was practically nonexistent. Heart disease in the 40- to 50-year-old age group is nine times as high in the United States as it is in Japan. Japan's diet is very low in fat. Twenty-five other cultures with low-fat diets were analyzed for the incidence of heart disease. All were found to have a low rate of death from cardiovascular disorders.

The question remained, Could the difference be explained by differing genetic factors? A study of Japanese who had emigrated to the United States and adopted our diet was undertaken. It was found that the Americanized Japanese had our high instances of heart problems.

In another study, the diets of animals were altered to increase their fat intake. When animals were left to their natural diet, the evidence of cardiovascular problems was nonexistent. A forced diet of fat introduced a high incidence of heart disease.

The evidence has become very persuasive that our diet is a primary cause of the great number of premature disabilities and deaths from heart disease.

The medical profession made numerous studies in the 1950s and 1960s in an attempt to find ways to minimize the risks of death or physical impairment caused by deteriorating cardiovascular systems. Individuals whose tests revealed high levels of cholesterol and fat in their blood had five times the risk of suffering a heart attack, as did those who had normal levels. Further studies showed that lowering the fat intake in the diet lowered the level of cholesterol in the blood, and the American public was warned about the dangers of high intakes of fat and sugar in their diet. Sugar, honey, molasses, and other simple carbohydrates are converted very rapidly into fats in the blood. Complex carbohydrates are also broken down in our digestive system into fat, but the process is much slower, and our body is able to utilize the fat as it is produced.

Hypertension

It is estimated that hypertension, or high blood pressure, affects one out of eight people in the United States. It is thought that the loss of elasticity in the walls of the arteries and the restriction of the flow of blood caused by the buildup of plaque can cause an elevation of pressure. These abnormal pressures can cause the blood vessels to rupture (aneurysms) or be damaged. The damage may occur in the kidneys, eyes, and/or other organs, leading to impairment in their proper functioning. A rupture in the brain results in a cerebral hemorrhage or stroke.

It has long been known (although the exact causes are still not clear) that a diet high in salt increases the probability that an individual will develop high blood pressure. In most instances a lowering of the intake of salt will result in a reduction of high blood pressure. As a nation we have increased our intake of processed foods, which generally have salt added. Consequently, even if little or no salt is added at the table, our intake of salt is still high.

Lack of Exercise

The heart is a muscle and needs exercise, just as all of our other muscles need exercise to maintain vigor. Mankind has evolved from the time when we needed to exercise vigorously (hunting or tilling) in order to obtain food and clothing for ourselves and family. Today, most earn their living through the use of their intellect and thus often lead sedentary lives. The result is that many do not exercise their heart muscle sufficiently to maintain its health. Studies show that we need to exercise the heart muscle vigorously several times a week for at least 20 to 30 minutes, if we expect it to remain healthy.

Smoking

The dangers that accompany the use of tobacco are so well known that little needs to be said about the advantages of not smoking. An individual who smokes increases the probability of developing lung cancer by 1000 percent over that of a nonsmoker. The dangers to smokers for contracting emphysema have also been established. Most people are not as aware of the increased danger smoking creates, as it relates to heart problems. Smokers have a 50 percent greater chance of experiencing heart trouble than do nonsmokers. In view of the higher number of deaths from heart attacks, it follows that cigarette smoking contributes to more deaths from heart attacks than from lung cancer.

Stress

Individuals who experience continuously high levels of stress appear to have a higher incidence of cardiovascular difficulties. The reasons for this are not entirely clear. It may be the involvement of physiological factors such as a constriction of the blood vessels. Or the problem may be due to the body's reaction to the introduction of adrenalin and other secretions into the bloodstream over a long period of time. A program dedicated to promoting wellness must include the controlling of the causes of stress. This subject will be dealt with in more depth in the next chapter.

PREPARING FOR A QUALITY LIFE

The purpose of this material has not been to provide medical advice. Rather, it has been to convince you that sufficient evidence exists to indicate that, for many of us, our life style is contributing to a needless decline in health in our later years and, too often, to premature death. Perhaps more important than our concern for the quantity of life, should be our consideration of the quality of life we will experience in later years.

If we wish to assure quality life in our retirement years, we need to avoid, or at least delay, the onslaught of degenerative diseases. I hope I have convinced you that how you choose to live in your early and middle years has a great influence on the quality of health you can expect in your later years. The tragedy is that due to the nature of degenerative diseases, we are usually unaware of the damages we are inflicting on our body until the degeneration has progressed to a level that creates permanent impairment. And, even though we are aware of the dangerous route we are following, we somehow believe it will not happen to us.

What should we do? For most of us, the answer is to recognize the dangers associated with our present life style and resolve to change. We should seek professional help. A personal physician who is as much concerned with promoting present and future wellness as he or she is in treating illness is a needed partner in our efforts to maintain a quality life.

When we purchase a new automobile, we are provided with an owner's manual. The manufacturer's engineers provide advice on how to use and maintain the car so that we will secure maximum, trouble-free miles. Unfortunately, whoever is responsible for the design and assembling of our beings did not issue an owner's manual for the care and maintenance of the vehicle we use to transport us through life. Perhaps it was not necessary in the early history of mankind, since the life style required for survival did not work at cross purposes with the genetic engineering conceived by the master designer.

However, that is not true today; and we need to construct an owners's manual for our bodies. It should cover the proper use and maintenance of our bodies, for that is the only vehicle we will be provided to convey us through life.

It is not necessary to understand all the engineering principles used in constructing your automobile in order to use and maintain it properly. Likewise, it is not necessary to completely understand the internal functioning of our bodies to maintain a state of wellness. It is sufficient that, with the help of your physician, you arrive at a life style that will assure your body is maintained properly.

Your concerns should include:

- Nutritional Intake
- Exercise Program
- Management of Emotions
- Abstinence from other harmful practices such as the use of tobacco and drugs

In the next chapter we will examine the subject of emotional health.

Chapter 3

Emotional Health

Emotional Health

Only by living can we hope to reach maturity. We have little control over our physical maturity. Sometime around the end of our second decade of life we stop growing and complete our physical development.

REACTIONS TO STRESS

There is no guarantee that the passing of years will result in our emotional maturity. An individual is perceived to have emotional health when able to cope successfully with the inevitable unpleasant occurrences encountered in the process of living. The individual is considered unsuccessful in coping when emotional pain seriously detracts from the quality of his or her life. Emotional pain is evidenced by such feelings as fear, anger, anxiety, and depression.

Emotional Pain

The experiencing of emotional pain is a necessary part of our existence. It signals that (1) a situation exists that represents a threat to us, and we should take some sort of action to avoid the danger or (2) our emotional response to an event in our life is incorrect. For example, a fear of heights may prevent us from venturing close to the edge of a cliff and thus prevent us from falling to our death. The same fear may exist when we fly in a commercial airplane. In the first case, the emotion can be avoided by keeping our distance from the edge of a precipice. If the fear of flying is so severe that it renders us incapable of air travel, however, it may be a major deterrent to our ability to live a normal life. The best solution would be to change the emotion (fear) associated with flying.

Individuals experiencing large amounts of stress often encounter problems with their physical health, in addition to their emotional pain. Modern society is often characterized as one in which we must cope with increasing amounts of stress. If we are to achieve a quality existence (wellness), we must learn how stress affects our physical body and what is involved in developing a stress management program.

The Fight or Flight Syndrome

In the early existence of mankind, survival depended on the ability to recognize and react appropriately to danger. For example, when early cave dwellers were confronted by a predatory monster, their survival depended upon their ability to react appropriately, either by fight or flight. They could elect to stand their ground and attempt to defeat the threat to survival, or they could flee and perhaps escape the danger.

To prepare them to accomplish either option, certain changes took place in their body. Their heartbeat quickened and their blood pressure rose. Adrenalin poured into their blood stream to speed the flow of blood sugar into their muscles and brain, giving them added strength to fight or flee. Their digestive system turned off so all of their energy could be directed to wherever needed. Blood vessels contracted to direct blood to the vital organs. The clotting ability of their blood was enhanced to reduce the loss of blood if they were injured. These, and other changes, occurred rapidly to assist them in meeting the challenge to their survival. If they were successful in meeting the challenge, either they destroyed or defeated the threat to their life, or they were successful in escaping. Normally, in a short period of time, the threat was over, and the functioning of their bodies returned to normal. One cannot help but marvel at the complexity and efficiency that the master designer built into the human machine.

Unfortunately, this design is not as appropriate in today's environment. When the threat is the boss, the same changes occur in our bodies, but we no longer have the same options. A punch in the nose somehow does not usually seem appropriate. Neither is quitting the job and fleeing. So while our body is prepared for "fight" or "flight," we select neither option but choose to stay and try to cope with the threat. Too often the threat continues, the body changes become a continuing state, and our body functions do not return to the norm conceived by our design engineer.

Illness

If, over an extended period of time, the abnormal becomes normal, then our physical and/or emotional health suffers. Based on our genetic makeup, we may experience one or more of the illnesses listed below:

Cardiovascular Ailments
    Heart attack
    Stroke
    Angina
    Irregular heartbeat
    Migraine headache
Digestive Ailments
    Ulcers
    Colitis
    Constipation
    Diarrhea
Immune System Failure
    Allergies
    Arthritis
    Various types of infections
    Cancer
Skeletal-Muscular Disorders
    Backache
    Tension headache
    Arthritis
    Asthma
    Proneness to accidents
Mental Problems
    Fear
    Anger
    Anxiety
    Depression
    Irritability
    Insomnia

STRESSFUL LIFE EVENTS

Doctors Holmes and Rahe, working at the University of Washington School of Medicine, have made some revealing findings in the studies on the effects of stress. They identified 43 life events that create stress and rated each according to the degree of adjustment required. The following table is the summary of their findings:

THE SOCIAL READJUSTMENT RATING SCALE

Rank	Life Event	Mean Value
1.	Death of spouse	100
2.	Divorce	73
3.	Marital separation	65
4.	Jail term	63
5.	Death of close family member	63
6.	Personal injury or illness	53
7.	Marriage	50
8.	Fired at work	47
9.	Marital reconciliation	45
10.	Retirement	45
11.	Change in health of family member	44
12.	Pregnancy	40
13.	Sex difficulties	39
14.	Gain of new family member	39
15.	Business adjustment	39
16.	Change in financial status	38
17.	Death of a close friend	37
18.	Change to a different line of work	36
19.	Change in number of arguments with spouse	35
20.	A large mortgage	31
21.	Foreclosure of mortgage or loan	30
22.	Change in responsibilities at work	29
23.	Son's or daughter's leaving home	29
24.	Trouble with in-laws	29
25.	Outstanding personal achievement	28
26.	Wife begins or stops work	26
27.	Begin or end of school	26
28.	Change in living conditions	25
29.	Revision of personal habits	24
30.	Trouble with boss	23
31.	Change in work hours or conditions	20
32.	Change in residence	20
33.	Change in schools	20
34.	Change in recreation	19
35.	Change in church activities	19
36.	Change in social activities	18
37.	Small mortgage or loan	17
38.	Change in sleeping habits	16
39.	Change in number of family get-togethers	15
40.	Change in eating habits	15
41.	Vacations	13
42.	Christmas	12
43.	Minor violation of the law	11

The stress causing events listed above are cumulative. As an example, let's assume that an individual loses his or her job. This alone creates a stress factor of 47. The job loss would result in a change in financial status (39). It could lead to a foreclosure on his or her home (30); perhaps an increase in the number of arguments with their spouse (35); and eventually a divorce (73). In reviewing the above table, you will find other changes that might result from the loss of a job. But, just from the events mentioned, the individual who lost his or her job would have to handle 224 units of stress.

Doctors Holmes and Rahe's studies also found that the higher number of adjustment factor units you acquire over a twelve-month period, the greater the probability that you will experience a serious health change during the coming year. The following table details the risk:

Adjustment Factor Points	Percent Chance of a Serious Health Change
Minimal	10%
150 or fewer	33%
150 to 300	50%
300 and above	80 to 90%

You have a ten-percent chance of having an illness serious enough to require a visit to the hospital without the added risks created by stress. As your cumulative stress factors increase, your chances of illness increase.

Many life events that create stress are not listed in the above table. For example, many experience considerable tension in preparing and giving a presentation before a large group. An Internal Revenue Department audit, deadlines to be met, and many everyday events bring that feeling of tightness which we all experience.

The assigned ratings by the doctors are only an approximation for an average individual. None of us is average. We each react differently to the events in our lives that create pressure.

The probability of illness is by no means a certainty. Depending upon our physical health and our ability to handle stress (our adaptive capacity), we have a widely varying capacity to handle the pressures of our life without experiencing health problems.

Later in this chapter we will review various methods of handling the tension-creating factors in our lives. But, first let's see how retirement may create stress.

RETIREMENT AS A SOURCE OF STRESS

Frequently individuals elect early retirement to escape the pressures experienced on the job. Others wait for mandatory retirement but look forward to a postretirement life style that is free from tension. In both cases, retirees are often surprised to experience new, and equally unpleasant, feelings of stress in their retirement life style.

We might predict that a newly retired individual will experience the stress factors listed in the table below.

Rank	Life Event	Scale of Impact
10.	Retirement	45
13.	Sex difficulties	39
16.	Change in financial status	39
19.	Change in number of arguments with spouse	35
28.	Change in living conditions	25
29.	Revision in personal habits	24
31.	Change in work hours	20
32.	Change in residence	20
34.	Change in recreation	19
35.	Change in church activities	19
36.	Change in social activities	18
38.	Change in sleeping habits	16
39.	Change in family get-togethers	15
40.	Change in eating habits	15
	TOTAL	349

Our hypothetical individual has an excellent chance of having a serious health problem within a year after retirement. Planning and scheduling could greatly reduce the health risks. Financial planning could minimize the change in the financial status. Improved communications with the spouse, prior to retirement, might eliminate the arguments. Maintaining preretirement routines after retirement would eliminate the change in sleeping, eating, and other personal habits. Remaining in the preretirement residence, for a least a time after retirement, could also reduce the accumulation of stress points.

POSTRETIREMENT STRESS

The above example (the stress-causing events accompanying retirement) deals with the transition to retirement. Once the transition is completed, won't the causes of stress disappear? Some will, but for many, others surface.

Boredom

One of the most typical is boredom. Studies have shown that industrial workers on tedious, repetitious assembly-line jobs evidenced very high levels of stress and suffered from symptoms of stress such as irritation and fatigue. It is sad but true that the life style of retirees has strong similarities to that of the production-line worker. On an assembly line, the worker repeats a series of meaningless, repetitious tasks. The workers endure their boredom because the Friday paycheck will enable them to provide the basic necessities of life for themselves and their family.

Many retirees repeat a series of meaningless, repetitious activities in an unsuccessful attempt to alleviate their boredom. Activities (such as golf, fishing, bridge, cocktail parties, or travel) that are undertaken simply to alleviate boredom fail to provide a zest for life. Often the retiree mistakenly believes the way to reduce the boredom is to speed up the production line. They mistakenly conclude that if they can cram more meaningless, repetitious activities into their schedule, they can reduce the pain that results from boredom. Such efforts, at best, usually bring only temporary relief.

Isolation

In some ways, retirees share common experiences with those individuals who are in solitary confinement. Individuals incarcerated in such an environment evidence extremely high levels of stress. It is typical for retirees to find that retirement separates them from social intercourse with their former co-workers. Those retirees experience a strong feeling of isolation because they no longer perceive that they have relationships that have meaning. Some try to go back and recapture past relationships, only to find that the interests of former associates and the retiree's interests are on ever-widening divergent paths. They become locked into the isolation of their innermost being. Even though they may be surrounded by others as they go about their daily activities, their spiritual essence is locked away in solitary isolation.

Role Ambiguity

Role ambiguity also creates stress. Within an organization, role ambiguity exists when there is a lack of clarity about the objectives expected of the position, and/or when associates' ideas of the worker's responsibilities differ from the worker's concept. Retirees who believe that their lives should have a purpose, while society considers them "over-the-hill has-beens," suffer stress similar to that experienced by individuals with role ambiguity in the corporate environment.

There are many other causes of stress associated with retirement. If suicide is caused by high levels of emotional pain, it might be concluded that for many, retirement is the most painful period of life. The suicide rate of individuals between the ages of 65 to 75 is higher than for any other ten-year period in our lifetime.

THE STRESS MANAGEMENT PROGRAM

An automobile engine needs fuel (gasoline) to propel it on its journey. The fuel, however, must be ingested into the motor in the proper proportions. Too lean of a mixture will make it impossible to start the engine. Too rich of a mixture will cause a sluggish operation of the motor, and the engine will stall if the accelerator is depressed for more power. A human being needs stress to operate efficiently. But, we need to experience it in the right proportions. Too little stress causes us to feel bored, lethargic, listless, and very possibly causes impairment of our bodily functions. Too much stress creates an overload on our adaptive capacity to handle stress. We can improve the quality of our lives if we develop a good stress management program. Each individual's program should be tailored to his or her specific needs.

The earlier in life you develop such a program, the greater the probability that you will enter retirement unscarred by emotional and/or physical disabilities. Your program will also serve you well in managing the stresses associated with retirement.

Your stress management program should include the following:

- An identification of those events in your life that are creating stress and an estimate of the amount of tensions that each such event is creating
- A prediction of future events that may occur in your life that will create stress and a review as to how those events can be handled to reduce undesirable emotional responses
- A plan to avoid stress-causing events when practical
- The scheduling (when possible) of situations which create tension, in such a manner as to keep the cumulative effects of stress within your adaptive capacity
- The development of techniques to increase your adaptive capacity

The following are some thoughts as to how you can go about developing a stress management program.

Identifying Stressful Events

Introspection and self-analysis will make it possible for you to identify the stress-creating events in your life. List the situations which create that feeling of tension. After completing your list, try to recall your reaction to each event. How tense did you feel? Were any of the stress symbols (such as irritability, insomnia, tension headaches, anxiety, or stomach disorders) evidenced?

Using a scale of 10 to 100, assign a value of 100 to the event that causes you the greatest stress. Give a value of 10 to the occurrence causing the least tension. To the other events on your list, assign values relative to your perception of their intensity as compared to the event receiving 100 and the one you gave a 10 rating. Your list should include stressful events you have actually experienced as well as those that can be considered a normal occurrence in your daily living. For example, you may find the preparation of your departments's budget and the presentation and defense of it before the budget committee very stressful. Even though it will only occur once a year, you should include it on your list. Do not attempt to make your ratings agree with those found on Doctors Holmes and Rahe's Social Adjustment Scale.

Predicting Future Stressful Events

This list should include the events you anticipate experiencing in the future that will be new, and which you have not experienced. The transitions in life can be expected to create stress. Entering the job market after graduating from school, marriage, the birth of a child, your midlife crises, and retirement are some of the transitions that you can predict will be accompanied by stress. If you anticipate that you will be facing such a change in the near future, the transitions can be made easier if you know what to expect. Literature is available about some of these changes, and it will give you some helpful pointers on what to expect. A friend or acquaintance who has experienced the transition can assist you in predicting some of your reactions to the change. Our emotional pain is often intensified during transition periods in our lives because we believe the pain is caused by our inadequacies. We do not understand that pain is a normal part of the process of reaching emotional maturity. This is especially true for men. The more macho the mask, the greater the pain. Most males have been conditioned to believe that grown men don't cry, and they keep their pain internalized. List those events of this type that you expect to experience in the next two years, and if possible, (maybe with the help of a friend who has experienced the event) assign them an impact rating.

Avoiding Pain

With a little planning we can avoid many of the stressful events in life. Retirees can avoid boredom by planning for meaningful activities during their retirement years. They can develop skills in making acquaintances, friends, and close friends and can thus avoid a feeling of isolation. The strengthening of one's self-image can minimize the problem of dealing with the stress associated with role ambiguity. (Methods of accomplishing an improved self-image have been discussed in Section II of this material.)

It might be wise to decline a position as head of the annual United Way fund drive immediately following your accepting a new position with your company. Perhaps trying to cope with the pain associated with both a divorce and a new job in a distant community will overload your adaptive capacity. Maybe you should postpone changing jobs until you have recovered from the stress associated with the breakup of the marriage.

Scheduling Pain

Many of the stress-creating events in our life can be scheduled. In the discussion of the stress associated with retirement, I gave an example of how we might elect to schedule the changes associated with retirement to avoid over-extending our adaptive capacity to handle stress.

Increasing Adaptive Capacity

Individuals vary widely in their capacity to handle stress without experiencing harmful side effects. The achievers and winners in life generally have the ability to handle high levels of stress. Some are fortunate in that they seem to have acquired this ability through their genetic heritage and/or early training. But each of us can learn to increase our adaptive capacity and thus equip ourselves to live life more fully and/or avoid impairment of our physical and emotional health. People who have a capacity for handling high levels of stress successfully usually have at least some, if not all, of the following characteristics.

Physical Vigor

Exercise is one of the finest methods of reducing stress. The experiencing of stress, as I have explained, ingests certain chemicals into our body to increase our ability to perform physical tasks. Exercise dissipates these chemicals and assists the body in returning to a normal state. Moreover, a healthy body can handle a heavier load of stress (without developing physical or mental health problems) than can a body allowed to become flabby through disuse. A fast game of tennis or handball or a brisk walk can reduce the feeling of tension and fatigue that follows a bad day at the office and leave one feeling vigorous, alive, and ready to meet the next day's challenges.

Mental Strength

A positive and confident attitude helps us meet many of the stressful events in our lives. Often we see two professional golfers arrive at the last few holes of a tournament tied for the lead. One sees the situation as an opportunity to win and begins to make exceptional shots and putts. The other begins to fear that he or she will lose, and his or her game falters. The difference is attitude. Some people go through life seeing problems (rather than opportunities) and develop the habit of choking. Others see mostly opportunities and establish the pattern of winning. Develop a positive mental attitude if you want to increase your ability to handle stress.

Successful handlers of stress are usually good problem solvers. Or, perhaps it is more accurate to say, they are good at identifying a problem. Before one can solve a problem, one must identify it. A poor solution applied to a correctly identified problem is not a total waste. At least you are beginning to identify what does not work. And you have the opportunity to try another solution, which may correct the problem.

Another dimension of problem solving is the development of options. If you can prevent it, do not let your solution to a problem paint you into a corner. Leave yourself an out. Even mild mannered animals will fight if they find themselves endangered and blocked from escape. You will view a stressful event differently if you perceive you have an optional solution to the problem.

We all have periods in our life when the severity of stressful events creates intense emotional pain. It helps to recognize that the crises will pass. A death of someone close to you, a divorce, the loss of a job will all bring pain. But with time, the pain will ease. The pain is intensified for the individual who feels his life is ruined forever. The person who understands that the pain will lessen with time, and who has faith that the future will be better, is less apt to suffer a serious impairment to his or her physical and/or emotional being.

It is important that we maintain stability zones in our lives. The individual who has a happy and well adjusted family relationship can handle much more job-related stress than the person who must contend with stress both at home and on the job. Examine your social life, your routines, your recreational activities, your personal habits, and your commute to work, to see if any are adding unnecessarily to your accumulated stress units.

When we are relaxed, our blood pressure drops, our heartbeat slows, muscle tension decreases, our respiratory rate slows, and our body chemistry is normal. That is what happened to our early ancestors after they defeated the saber tooth tiger that was chasing them. If modern men and women could relax after the boss "chewed them out," they wouldn't experience nearly as many stress-related illnesses. There are many different types of relaxation techniques that can be learned and practiced. It is important that the techniques produce the above mentioned bodily changes and do not just result in our lying quietly but still tense with that tight feeling inside. Various muscle relaxation techniques, such as meditation, self-hypnosis, and bio-feedback, have been proven to be effective in bringing true relaxation to certain individuals. The adoption of some form of relaxation technique should be an integral part of every stress management program.

Spiritual Vitality

An individual's adaptive capacity for stress is aided by a strong sense of his or her spiritual being. The subject is covered more fully in the next chapter. For now, let it suffice for me to point out that such an individual displays at least some of the following characteristics:

- Possessing an outward, rather than an inward, focus
- Feeling in control of one's life
- Living a life that is in harmony with one's values
- Believing that one is loved and worthwhile
- Experiencing the attainment of creative goals

In summary, we all experience stress in our lives; and if the amount of stress exceeds our adaptive capacity, we are apt to experience physical and emotional problems. In order to live more fully, we should develop a stress management program that is uniquely tailored to our individuality.

Chapter 4
Spiritual Health

Spiritual Health

Each of us is the creator of our own destiny. We use our physical body and our intellect to convey our being from the beginning to the end of our journey.

A passenger occupies the body and uses the intellect to influence the destination and the quality of the trip. The passenger is our spiritual dimension, which we will call **YOU**.

THE UNIVERSALITY OF BELIEF

Mankind, from the earliest recorded history, has been intrigued by the YOU that resides in the human species. Philosophers, theologians, and intellectuals have explored the essence of our being and attempted to convey their perceptions as to the nature and purpose of YOU. Different cultures and races have arrived at widely different concepts as to the existence and meaning of our spiritual being. Nations have been founded, wars fought, and persecution and genocide practiced due to these differences. The universality as to the sense of the existence of YOU suggests that an essential part of our humanity is a preprogrammed knowledge that such a dimension exists in the human race.

In addition to a sense of the YOU in each of us, mankind has throughout history attempted to identify and describe the existence of a universal intelligence. We will call it **IT**. Our beliefs in the existence and the nature of IT, and its relationship with YOU, influence our concepts as to how we modify the vehicle conveying YOU, to optimize the satisfaction and purpose of our existence.

UNDERSTANDING OUR BEING

In spite of the tremendous progress throughout the centuries in science and technology, we have made little, if any, progress in establishing scientific proof as to the nature and relationship of YOU and IT. Perhaps it is presumptuous for the finite to attempt to define the infinite. Faith alone, may be the only foundation we will ever have to formulate whatever beliefs we hold as to the nature of our spiritual being.

While sciences have given us only a limited ability to know and understand the YOU segment of our existence, it has given us an increasingly clear picture of the vehicle provided us for our journey. We have acquired extensive knowledge about the various organs of our physical body, and we even know how to repair, and in some instances, replace them. We can identify all the bones in our skeleton and replace worn-out joints. We are familiar with all of our muscles and understand which ones contract and which relax when we move the various parts of our body. We have a good knowledge of the chemistry of the body, how to nurture it properly, and how to help it fight disease. We know which parts of the brain are used for various purposes. We have substantially increased the expected length of our voyage, and our knowledge is growing exponentially.

We have made less progress in understanding our intellect and little, if any, progress in helping mankind use it better. The rising uses of alcohol and mood-altering drugs, the increasing need for psychiatric care, increases in suicides, increasing crime and divorce rates — all suggest that the life's voyage for an increasing portion of our population is extremely painful. We have not learned to manage our intellect so as to improve the quality of our life. We are not programming our central processing unit (our brain) properly. Our YOU has not learned to take charge of our life.

THE PROGRAMMING OF OUR INTELLECT

Our brain is a part of our physical body and the source of our intellect. When we enter this world, we come equipped with a brain partially preprogrammed. We are programmed to breathe; and our heart beats, our digestive system functions, our garbage disposal system works. If we get hot, we sweat; and, within limits, our built-in air conditioning system keeps our bodies at a constant temperature. The brain maintains our body chemistry, and our bodies are able to fight off most invading viruses.

Immediately we start programming our intellect. We gain the ability to focus our eyes and to recognize familiar faces. We learn to control our muscles and to crawl, then walk and talk. We learn to express thought, first in words and then sentences. We learn to recognize symbols and to read. We use our input devices (our eyes, ears, nose, taste buds, and nerve endings) to provide us information. And we write programs for our intellect so that these inputs will result in predictable outputs. Some of these outputs are in the form of emotions, such as love, joy, happiness, fear, anger, or anxiety. The YOU in each of us writes the programs; and depending upon the program we write, we will have predictable outputs from certain inputs. For example, one baby being tossed in the air and caught by the father may be programmed to produce fear, while another may react to the same experience with joy and laughter.

There are widely divergent beliefs as to the role YOU plays in these programming efforts. One school of thought insists that our YOU has little influence on the programs written. They believe that our genetic inheritance, the environment, and parental nurturing (or lack thereof) controls the programming of the intellect, and that we are destined to take life's journey with the outputs almost solely conditioned by the events we experience during our first few years of life. Many individuals make their way through a life with constant pain because they are convinced they have been programmed to a life of misery and that they have little, if any, control over their destiny. At the other end of this spectrum is the belief that our YOU has complete control over our destiny. Every misfortune, illness, accident, and sorrow occurs because we willed it to happen, albeit subconsciously. In other words, according to that school of thought, even the tragedies that occur to each of us happen because our YOU willed them to happen. The truth probably lies somewhere between these two extremes.

REPROGRAMMING OUR INTELLECT

In our early years our YOU is undeveloped and weak, and external circumstances greatly influence the programming of our intellect. The process of living and maturing consists of reexamining our programs; and where existing programs are inappropriate, we should reprogram ourselves for a more appropriate output to the inputs we receive as the events of our life unfold. Erich Fromm said: "Living is the process of continuous rebirth."

How do we know whether our intellect is programmed correctly? We know by the outputs that result from our inputs. Anxiety, depression, fear, tension, and other forms of emotional pain are indicators that we need to examine our program if the emotion is improper, considering the input. For example, the fear of all bosses would probably be considered inappropriate, and reprogramming would be called for. On the other hand, the fear of a sadistic, egotistical boss might be perfectly normal, and a change of the input (working for such a boss) might be the logical solution. If an event results in an output of love, joy, happiness, and/or an increased sense of self-worth, it is an indicator that we are correctly programmed to respond to the event that is creating that output.

In order to reprogram our intellect, there needs to be a strong sense of the existence of, and the power of, a YOU within us. It is helpful if one also senses the existence of IT and believes that a relationship exists between IT and YOU. It is also helpful if one believes that there is a grand scheme in existence in which YOU has a role to play.

The existence of pain in your life is easy to detect. It is often extremely difficult to identify the input that is creating the pain. Daily we receive many inputs which create a variety of emotional responses, and the inputs and responses often react and interact with each other. An individual could have multiple problems at the same time: disenchantment with the job, arguments with the spouse, and problems with the children. All cause pain. Which are the causative problems? Is the job creating the pain, which then results in problems with the boss, spouse, and children? Or, is the marriage the primary problem? Perhaps it is none of these, but rather a growing dependence upon alcohol. Most of us will experience such periods of crises in our lives. Only through arduous introspection and self-analysis can we correctly identify the primary causes of our distress. We are apt to act impulsively and, if we are not careful, may be tempted to quit our job, get a divorce, or take some other inappropriate action in lashing out to relieve our pain. A friend with whom to talk out the problem may be of help. Or, the pain may be so severe and the solution so complex that the use of professional help is needed.

The skill required to reprogram ourselves effectively can be learned. And with practice we can improve our reprogramming skills. It is easier to handle a simple reprogramming effort than a complex one. An unresolved programming error is apt to lead to increasing pain and an increasingly complex problem to be dealt with later.

FORMULATING OUR ULTIMATE CONCERN

A major dilemma many of us face is that we do not know just what we want our programmed intellect to achieve. We know what we want to avoid, pain. But we have no yardstick against which to measure the successes of our intellectual programming efforts. Perhaps the most important question we can ask ourselves is, What is my ultimate concern? Be careful in arriving at your answer. It is easy to delude one's self. Many people will say, "I want to be happy." Don't we all! They think, "I will be happy if I have an automobile." So they get one and are happy for a short time; and then they want a boat. Next, they want a bigger car, a nicer home, and hence they are never satisfied. Their life is filled with moments of pseudo-happiness, interspersed with lengthy periods of wanting more. Narcissistic practices do not bring happiness.

Happiness comes from being and acting unselfishly. One must have a sense of self-worth and a belief that he or she has the ability to contribute to the happiness of other human beings. We get more satisfaction from freely giving than from receiving.

Ultimate concerns for power, fame, affluence, or prestige are false gods if they become the primary focus of our lives.

WORKING TOWARD WELLNESS

Once you have formulated your ultimate concern and correctly identified your cause of pain, the process of reprogramming your intellect can begin. But it is not an easy process. Our habits of processing information are usually well ingrained and difficult to change. Those of you who play golf know how easy it is to develop faults in your basic swing. A golfing professional can usually identify the faults and work with you until they are eliminated. Your shots on the practice range become marvels to observe. But all too often, back on the course, head-to-head with your Saturday foursome, all your faults reappear and the old habits return. When new muscular habits are to replace old muscular habits, one must practice until the new replaces the old.

Studies have shown that we can improve our muscular abilities by imagining improvement. Most golf and tennis professionals include mental conditioning as a part of their teaching lessons.

It has also been found that we can change our emotional outputs by changing how we perceive situations. For example, some individuals are gripped by fear at the thought of getting up before a group to make a presentation. In an imaging session, several such individuals practiced imagining themselves making a presentation in front of a group. They visualized themselves as confident, proficient, articulate, and successful. After practicing their imagery for a period of time, they actually made the types of successful presentations they had performed in their imagination.

You can reprogram yourself. The YOU in us does want to succeed. Prove to yourself that reprogamming does work. Take a simple reprogramming task. Practice mentally succeeding for several days. Then accomplish something that you found difficult or impossible before. Take control of your life and achieve your ultimate concern. Achieve a high level of spiritual wellness. Just remember that spiritual health consists of a knowledge of and the skill to use the power of YOU to achieve your ultimate concern.

Please review the following chart.

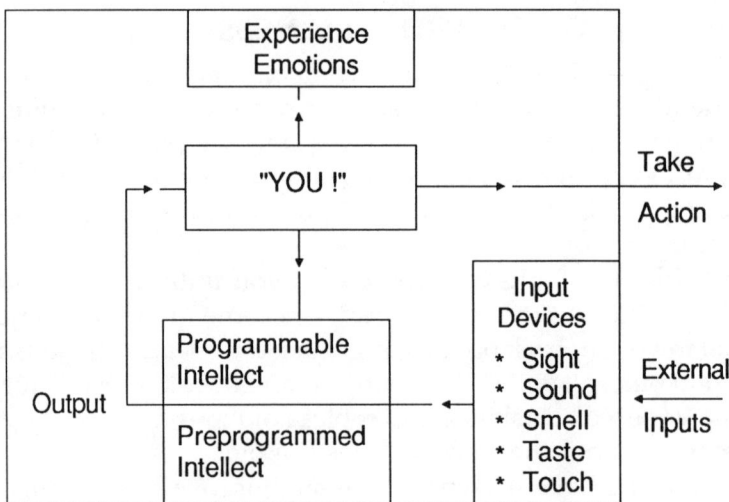

Chapter 5

Your Plan for Wellness

Your Plan for Wellness

I suspect it is a rare individual who has attained the optimum physical, emotional, and spiritual health. Most of us can, however, improve our sense of wellness. The purpose of this chapter is to give you some thoughts on how you can construct a plan for wellness.

DETERMINING YOUR PRESENT CONDITION

As in financial planning, we must first determine where we are. Sections A through D of WS-III.5.1 encourage the self-analysis and introspection required to determine your present state of wellness. The next step is to determine where you want to go. The ability to achieve a one (1) rating for each of the categories on the Wellness Profile (Section D. of WS-III.5.1) is a laudable goal.

PLANNING FOR IMPROVEMENT

You should now be ready to formulate your plan for improving your wellness. I suggest you approach your plan in the inverse order in which the topics were covered in this section of the book. It is doubtful that one can long sustain physical health unless a fairly high degree of emotional health is maintained. Many physicians estimate that over 50 percent of their patients seek their services because of a psychosomatic illness. I suspect that the ratio for retirees is higher than for the general population. The older population occupies bodies that frequently have suffered many years of trauma from high levels of stress. In addition, the elderly are more imminently confronted with the finiteness of life than are the young, and thus they are more apprehensive about any symptoms of health disorder.

It is doubtful if one can achieve a high level of emotional maturity unless one has come to some understanding about his or her spiritual nature. People who do not like themselves find it impossible to like others. If you do not love yourself, you cannot love your neighbor. I suggest, therefore, that you give top priority to the development of your spiritual being, then your emotional maturity, and finally your physical health.

Establishing Goals

You will probably want to establish goals in each of these areas. Select your goals carefully. Someone once said that there are two tragedies in life. The first is having a goal and never achieving it. The second is having a goal and achieving it.

In the first instance, the failure to reach a goal may well result in an individual's believing that his or her life is a failure. In the second, the individual who reaches his or her life's goal may feel that life has no further purpose.

The solution is to establish a series of intermediate goals. As you achieve the first, you experience the satisfaction of achievement and concurrently benefit from the challenge of the next goal in your hierarchy of objectives. Changing human nature is difficult. Therefore, incorporate as many motivational tools as possible into your plan.

Updating Annually

It would be beneficial to update your assessment of the degree of your wellness and your plan for improvement on an annual basis. By comparing your level of attainment from year to year, you can sense your progress.

Retirement is a continuation of all of your previous existence; and the less garbage (in the form of physical and emotional problems) you bring to this point in your life, the more joyful will be your golden years. Also the skills you develop in coping will serve you well as you experience the stress of the retirement transition. Complete WS-III.5.1.

You now have plans to achieve financial security, a purpose for your life, and wellness in your retirement. Face the future confidently and expect that the best is yet to be: the last of life for which the first was made.

Conclusions

If you have faithfully and carefully completed all the work sheets, you probably have invested 70 to 80 hours in preparing your plan for retirement. You can expect to have some 76,000 waking hours during retirement. Your ratio of retirement planning to retirement living is 1/10 of 1 percent. Applying the same ratio of planning for a two-week vacation would result in your allotting yourself 12 minutes of preparation. Few of us would consider endangering our enjoyment of a two-week holiday by such skimpy preparation. However, many, perhaps most, enter retirement with little if any planning.

The time you spent in retirement planning will be largely wasted if it is not followed by implementation. To accomplish the changes outlined in your plan, you must devote time and effort in assuring yourself that your road map to the future is actually being followed.

There are at least three pitfalls that I would urge you to avoid.

1. Don't become so mesmerized by your plan that you fail to recognize changing conditions that may make it advisable to alter your projected course of action. Remain flexible and, if conditions change, change your plan as appropriate. Always consider your plan as a tool to be used in accomplishing your objectives, rather than an end in itself.
2. Don't become so engrossed in planning for the future that you forget your existence is always in the present. Some individuals become so engrossed with preparing for the future that they never pause to enjoy the present.
3. Don't become discouraged and abandon your plan. When we plan, we generally perceive a linear progression from where we are to where we want to be. But actual results seldom follow that path. Results may seem to plateau. However, with persistance and patience, progress should follow and you will achieve your goals.

The refrain of an old Scottish song says, "You take the high road and I'll take the low road, and I'll be in Scotland before ya." I think that is bad advice if you try to apply it to our life's journey. Who wants to be there first? It is the quality of the trip, not the speed that counts. The high road is a more pleasant place to travel.

We all start life's journey in the same way. And we all end our voyages in a like manner. It is the roads we choose to travel during our pilgrimage that determine our uniqueness.

All through life we encounter forks in the road that offer us choices. Some paths lead to the high road, others to the low road. At first glance the low road is often more inviting. The path to the low road gives us an opportunity to coast. It is easy to traverse and requires a minimum of effort. The majority of our traveling companions seem to be selecting that option. So, without a great deal of thought, we too elect the easy and popular route.

But all too frequently we are disappointed with the result. We find ourselves traveling in the shadows of life with little sunlight or scenery. The road is congested with traveling companions that are grumpy and dissatisfied.

It is never too late to select the high road. Throughout life, we are faced with numerous forks in the road. The earlier in life we elect to follow the high road, the greater the portion of our journey that will be spent experiencing a self-actualized life.

Each of us must determine the type of journey we wish to experience. And then we must evaluate each fork in the road to determine whether it leads to or away from our objectives. And we must be willing to pay the price to achieve our goals.

Retirement is just one of the forks in the road. If we arrive at this transition point with financial security, a purpose for our lives, and with good physical, emotional, and spiritual health, the transition should be easy and the balance of the time we have on this earth, enjoyable. We will truly be at the summit of our existence.

If you reach retirement having followed the low road, do not despair. You can still choose the high road. The climb will take effort, but the view from the summit is worth it.

Bibliography and Recommended Reading

The following is a partial list of the books that I read and studied, prior to writing this material.

All are recommended reading and would be of value in helping individuals prepare their plan for retirement. However, it is recognized that the constraints of time will limit most readers ability to read all of the books. Seven books have been marked with asterisks as they are considered to be the most relevant.

I do not endorse all of the ideas and concepts contained in the references. Some with differing viewpoints are included as an encouragement to readers to broaden their viewpoints and look at different alternatives. The emphasis throughout this material is for each individual to explore and come up with their individuality and to develop a plan that will best serve their uniqueness.

I am indebted to several publications that have carried many excellent articles that have been helpful. Special thanks are due to the *Wall Street Journal, Los Angeles Times, Newsweek, Modern Maturity,* and *The Readers Digest.*

Also a word of thanks is due my wife Lucille and two daughters, Barbara Stodder and Diane Holder, for their help in editing the material. I am greatly indebted to the many retired associates and friends who have read various drafts of the material and from their experience offered suggestions for changes, which usually have been adopted.

I take full responsibility, and accept the accountability, for the quality and relevance of the final product. My personal experience in coping with retirement could not help but influence the material and the recommended planning processes.

GENERAL

The Best Years Book *
  Hugh Downs & Richard J. Roll
  Delacorte Press/Eleanor Friede
  1 Dag Hammerskjold Plaza
  New York, N.Y. 10017

The Retirement Handbook
  Joseph C. Buckley revised by Henry Schmidt
  Fourth revised and enlarged edition
  Harper & Row Publishers Inc.
  49 East 33rd St.
  New York, N.Y. 10016

Plan Your Retirement Now So You Won't be Sorry Later
  U.S. News & World Report Inc.
  2300 N. Street N.W.
  Washington, D.C. 20037

How to Avoid the Retirement Trap
  Leland Fredrick Colley & Lee Morrison Colley
  Nash Publishing
  Los Angeles, Calif.

The Retirement Book
  Joan Adler
  William Morrow & Company, Inc.
  New York, N.Y.

Aging is Not for Sissies
  Terry Schuman
  The Westminister Press
  Philadelphia, Pa.

FINANCIAL SECURITY

The Intelligent Investor *
  Benjamin Graham
  Fourth Revised Edition
  Harper & Row, Publishers
  New York, Evanston, San Francisco, London

Money Dynamics for the 1980s *
  Venita Van Caspel
  Reston Publishing Company, Inc.
  A Prentice-Hall Company
  Reston, Virginia 22090

Personal Money Management
  Thomas E. Ballard, David L. Biehl, Ronald W. Kaiser
  Science Research Associates, Inc.
  Chicago, Illinois

Sylvia Porter's Money Book
  How to Earn it, Spend it, Save it, Invest it, Borrow it and Use it to Better Your Life
  Sylvia Porter
  Doubleday & Company, Inc.
  Garden City, New York

J. K. Lasser's Managing Your Family Finances
  J. K. Lasser Tax Institute
  Doubleday & Company, Inc.
  Garden City, New York

Tax Shelters and Tax-Free Income for Everyone
  William C. Drollinger
  Epic Publications
  Orchard Lake, Mich.

Survive & Win in the Inflationary Eighties
  Howard J. Ruff
  Warner Books
  75 Rockefeller Plaza
  New York, N. Y. 10019

The Dow Jones-Irwin Guide to Interest
  What You Should Know About the Time Value of Money
  Lawrence R. Rosen
  Dow Jones-Irwin, Inc.
  Homewood, Illinois 60430

LIFE WITH A PURPOSE

The Sky's the Limit *
  Dr. Wayne Dyer
  Simon and Schuster
  New York, N.Y.

Psycho-Cybernetics *
  Maxwell Maltz, M.D. F.I.C.S.
  Wilshire Book Company
  12015 Sherman Road
  North Hollywood, Ca. 91605

The Road Less Traveled
   A. Scott Peck, M.D.
   A Touchstone Book
   Simon and Schuster
   New York, N.Y.

How to Stop Worrying and Start Living
   Dale Carnegie
   Pocket Books
   New York, N.Y.

Your Erroneous Zones
   Dr. Wayne Dyer
   Funk & Wagnalls
   New York, N.Y.

Beyond Freedom and Dignity
   B. F. Skinner
   A Bantam/Vintage Book
   New York, N.Y.

Games People Play
   Eric Berne, M.D.
   Grove Press, Inc.
   New York, N.Y.

Transactional Awareness
   J. Allyn Bradford and Reuben Guberman
   Addison-Wesley Publishing Company
   Reading, Massachusetts

The O.K. Boss
   Muriel James
   Addison-Wesley Publishing Company
   Reading, Massachusetts

How to Talk with People
   Irving J. Lee
   Harper & Brothers, Publishers
   New York, N.Y.

WELLNESS

Live Longer Now
The First One Hundred Years of Your Life *
  Jon N. Leonard, J.L. Hofer, and N. Pritkin
  Charter Books
  360 Park Avenue South
  New York, N.Y. 10010

Managing Stress *
  Jere E. Yates
  Amacom
  A Division of American Management Associations
  135 West 50th St.
  New York, N.Y. 10020

Anatomy of an Illness as Perceived by the Patient
  Norman Cousins
  W. S. Norton & Company
  New York, N.Y.

There's a Lot More to Health Than Not Being Sick
  Bruce Larson
  World Book Publishers
  Waco, Texas

The Disowned Self
  Nathaniel Brandon
  Batam Books
  666 Fifth Ave.
  New York, N.Y. 10019

* Books considered most relevant

Appendix
Work Sheets

Section I
Financial Independence

Chapter 1 — Facts
WS-I.1.1   Net Worth 233
WS-I.1.2   Skill Inventory 234
WS-I.1.3   Retirement Lifestyle 235
WS-I.1.4   Retirement Housing 236

Chapter 2 — Assumptions
WS-I.2.1   Assumptions 237

Chapter 3 — Your Plan — Preretirees
WS-I.3.1   Personal Expense Budget 238
WS-I.3.2   Income Tax Due on Pension & Social Security 239
WS-I.3.3   Financial Plan for Retirement 242

Chapter 4 — Your Plan — Retirees
WS-I.4.1   Personal Expense Budget 244
WS-I.4.2   Financial Plan for Retirement 245

Chapter 5 — Investment Alternatives and Strategies
WS-I.5.1   Investment Alternatives and Strategies 247

Chapter 6 — Contingency and Alternative Plans
WS-I.6.1   Contingency and Alternative Plans 249

Chapter 7 — Monitoring Progress
WS-I.7.1   Monitoring Progress 250

Section II
Life With a Purpose

Chapter 2 — On Becoming a Retiree
WS-II.2.1 My Transition to Retirement 251

Chapter 3 — Reach Out and Touch Someone
WS-II.3.1 Social Skills Inventory 254

Chapter 4 — The Gap is the Problem
WS-II.4.1 My Self-Esteem Gap 256

Chapter 5 — Who am I?
WS-II.5.1 My Reason for Being 258

Chapter 6 — Why am I?
WS-II.6.1 Tactical Plan 260

Section III
Wellness

Chapter 5 — Your Plan for Wellness
WS-III.5.1 Evaluation of My State of Wellness
and My Plan for Improvement 262

WS-I.1.1.

NET WORTH

Name _____   Date _____

ASSETS   **LIABILITIES**

Cash & Checking Acct. $ _____   Charge Acct. Over
                                         30 Days Past Due $ _____

Savings Account $ _____

Stocks and Bonds $ _____   Loans $ _____
Profit Sharing Acct.
 & Deferred Comp. $ _____   Installment Cntr. $ _____

Cash Value of Ins. $ _____   Mortgages $ _____

Real Estate $ _____   Other (Specify below)

Home (mkt. value) $ _____   _____ $ _____
                                        _____ $ _____
Personal Property   _____ $ _____
 Automobiles $ _____   _____ $ _____
 Hshld. Furn. $ _____   _____ $ _____
 Furs, Jewelry, etc. $ _____   _____ $ _____
 Clothing $ _____   _____ $ _____
 Hobby Equip. $ _____

                                        Total Liabilities $ _____
Other (Specify below)
_____ $ _____
_____ $ _____
_____ $ _____
_____ $ _____
_____ $ _____

Total Assets $ _____
Less
Total Liabilities $ _____

NET WORTH $ _____

Inheritance
Anticipated $ _____

Adjusted Net Worth $ _____

WS-I.1.2

SKILL INVENTORY

Date: _____

Husband's Skills

1. _____
2. _____
3. _____
4. _____
5. _____
6. _____
7. _____

Wife's Skills

1. _____
2. _____
3. _____
4. _____
5. _____
6. _____
7. _____

WS-I.1.3

RETIREMENT LIFESTYLE
Recreation Desired

Husband	Wife
1. _____	1. _____
2. _____	2. _____
3. _____	3. _____
4. _____	4. _____
5. _____	5. _____

Intellectual Needs

1. _____	1. _____
2. _____	2. _____
3. _____	3. _____
4. _____	4. _____
5. _____	5. _____

Spiritual Needs

1. _____	1. _____
2. _____	2. _____
3. _____	3. _____
4. _____	4. _____
5. _____	5. _____

Mission of Life

Husband _____

_____

_____

_____

Wife _____

_____

_____

_____

WS-I.1.4

RETIREMENT HOUSING

YOUR PRESENT HOME

    Value of House and Lot $ _____

    Value of Lot   _____

    Value of House Only   _____

    Square Feet of House   _____

    Value of House Per Square Foot   _____

RETIREMENT HOME

    Square Feet Desired   _____

    Square Foot Cost   _____

    Cost of House Only   _____

    Cost of Lot   _____

    Cost of House and Lot   _____

FINANCING RETIREMENT HOME

    Total Cost $ _____

    Down Payment   _____

    Amount of Mortgage   _____

    Annual Mortgage Payments   _____

WS-I.2.1

ASSUMPTIONS

Assumed Long-Term Inflation Rate
   Before Retirement   _____ %
   After Retirement   _____ %
Assumed Earning Power of Lowest
   Risk Investments   _____ %
Assumed Future National Policy of
   Indexing Social Security Benefits   _____ %

CAREER PROGRESSION LEVEL

I will remain at my present level   Yes( )   No( )

I will advance _____ more levels

I want to retire at age _____ at which time I will have _____ years of service.

AGE ATTAINED BY ANCESTORS

	HUSBAND	WIFE
Mother's Father		
Mother's Mother		
Mother		
Father's Father		
Father's Mother		
Father		
Total		
MY GENERIC AGE (1)		

MY HEALTH HABITS

	HUSBAND	WIFE
Weight		
Smoke		
Stress		
Diet		
Salt Intake		
Total (2)		

ESTIMATED LONGEVITY (3)   _____   _____

NOTE: Determine the items numbered above as (1), (2), and (3) by the following formulas:
   (1) Divide total number by the number of deceased ancestors
   (2) Add or subtract 1 (one) for how you rate yourself for each of the health habits
   (3) Generic age plus or minus total of your health habits

WS-I.3.1

PERSONAL EXPENSE BUDGET

Prepared for: _____

Date: _____

	Current (A)	Cost Today If Retired (B)
HOUSING		
Mortgage Payment or Rent	$ _____	$ _____
Taxes and Insurance	_____	_____
Upkeep	_____	_____
Utilities	_____	_____
TOTAL HOUSING EXPENSE	$ _____	$ _____
FOOD		
Groceries & Misc.	$ _____	$ _____
Dining Out	_____	_____
TOTAL FOOD	$ _____	$ _____
CLOTHING		
New Clothes	$ _____	$ _____
Cleaning	_____	_____
TOTAL CLOTHING	$ _____	$ _____
TRANSPORTATION		
Car Payments & Insurance	$ _____	$ _____
Gas, Oil, & Maintenance	_____	_____
Other Transportation	_____	_____
TOTAL TRANSPORTATION	$ _____	$ _____
RECREATION		
Vacation & Travel	$ _____	$ _____
Other Recreation	_____	_____
TOTAL RECREATION	$ _____	$ _____
LIFE INSURANCE	$ _____	$ _____
MEDICAL & MEDICAL INSURANCE	$ _____	$ _____
GIFTS & CHARITIES	$ _____	$ _____
MISCELLANEOUS EXPENSES	$ _____	$ _____
OTHER EXPENSES	$ _____	$ _____
TOTAL EXPENSES	$ _____	$ _____

INFL.-FREE EXPENSES $ _____

INFL.-IMPACTED EXPENSES $ _____

WS-I.3.2
Page 1

INCOME TAX DUE ON PENSION

FEDERAL INCOME TAX (F.I.T.) DUE ON PENSION

(1) Estimated Pension in Today's Dollars $ _____
     (See note below)

(2) Itemized Deductions (Est. at time of retirement)   _____

(3) Net (line 1 minus line 2)   _____

(4) Personal Deductions   _____

(5) Taxable Income from Pension only (L3 - L4)   _____

(6) Tax (Use Tax Table)   _____

     $ _____ plus __% of ($ _____ minus $ _____)   _____

CALIFORNIA STATE INCOME TAX (S.I.T.) DUE ON PENSION

(7) Estimated Pension in Today's Dollar $ _____
     (See note below)

(8) Itemized Deductions (Est. at time of retirement)   _____

(9) Net (line 7 minus line 8)   _____

(10) Tax (Use Tax Table)   _____

     $ _____ plus __% of ($ _____ minus $ _____)   _____

(11) Personal Deductions   _____

(12) Net Tax (line 10 minus line 11)   _____

(13) TOTAL INCOME TAX DUE ON PENSION (L6 + L12) $ _____

NOTE: Itemized Deductions on Line 2 and Line 8 above would be the amount you would show on Line 26 of Schedule A of the Federal Return and Line 33 of Schedule NR A of the California State Return.

WS-I.3.2
Page 2

FEDERAL INCOME TAX DUE ON SOCIAL SECURITY BENEFIT

(14) One-Half of Your Est. Annual Value
Soc. Sec. Bnft. in Today's Dollars
(See Note 1, next page) $ _____

(15) Est. Value of All Other Sources of Income
at Time of Retirement in Today's Dollars
(Include pension, investment income, etc.)
(See note 2, next page)   _____

(16) Total Income (Line 14 + Line 15)   _____

(17) Itemized Deductions (Est. at time of retirement)   _____

(18) Personal Deductions   _____

(19) Net Income (Line 15 minus Line 16 plus Line 17)   _____

(20) Base Amount Above Which a Portion of Soc. Sec.
Benefit Is Taxable ($32,000 joint or $25,000
individual filing)   _____

(21) Compare Line 19 with Line 20.
If Line 19 is less than Line 20   NO TAX IS DUE
If Line 19 is more than Line 20 show difference   _____

(22) Taxable Social Security Benefit
(Line 21 times 50%)   _____

(23) Applicable Tax Rate (Line 6, page 1.)   _____ %

(24) Federal Income Tax on Soc. Sec. Bnft.
(Line 22 times Line 24)   _____

(25) TOTAL INCOME TAX DUE ON PENSION
AND SOCIAL SECURITY BENEFIT
(ADD LINES 13 AND 24) $ _____
SHOW THE ABOVE AMOUNT ON WS-I.3.3, LINE 7.

WS-I.3.2
Page 3

NOTE 1. If you had paid the maximum Social Security tax each year and reached the age of 65 in 1984, you would be entitled to a maximum benefit of $703 per month or $8,436 annually. If you chose to receive your benefit at 62, the amount you would be entitled to receive would be 80% of the maximum benefit or $6,748. A spouse at age 65 would be entitled to 50% of the primary benefit. If you have paid less than the maximum Social Security tax in the past or you will have less than 35 years of coverage by the time you retire, a visit to the local Social Security office will enable you to obtain literature that will assist you in estimating your future benefit stated in the value of today's dollars.

NOTE 2. A portion of your Social Security benefit may be subject to Federal Income tax if your income from your pension, investment income (including tax free income) and one-half of your Social Security benefit exceeds $25,000 for an individual or $32,000 for those filing jointly. In order to estimate whether a portion of your Social Security benefit will be taxable, it will be necessary for you to make an estimate of the amount of income you will receive from investments at the time of your retirement.

WS-I.3.3
Page 1

FINANCIAL PLAN
FOR RETIREMENT

Name _____   Date _____

			Base Year
Line	**RETIREMENT BUDGET**		
1.	INCOME		
2.	Pension		$ _____
3.	Soc. Sec.		_____
4.	Total Income	L2 + L3	_____
5.	EXPENSE		
6.	Inflation Free		_____
7.	Inc. Tx. (Pens. & Soc. Sec.)		_____
8.	Inflation-Impacted		_____
9.	Total Expense	L6 + L7 + L8	_____
10.	DEFICIT OR SURPLUS	L4 - L9	$ _____

	INVESTMENT REQUIRED		Factor(1)	
11.	To Cover First-Year Deficit	L10/factor	_____	$ _____
12.	To Cover Incr. Infl.-Impacted Exp.			
13.	Impacted Expense Only	L8 x factor	_____	_____
14.	If Aft-Tx Earn is not = Infl.	L13 x factor	_____	_____
15.	Soc. Sec. Contribution	L3 x factor	_____	_____
16.	Net Required	L14 - L15		_____
17.	First-Year Surplus Contribution	L10/factor	_____	(_____)
18.	TOTAL INVESTMENT REQUIRED	L16 + L11 or L16 - L17		_____

	YOUR PLAN			
19.	Existing Investments			$ _____
20.	Investments at Time of Retirement	L19 x factor	_____	_____
21.	Excess (Shortage) of Investments	L20 - L18		_____
22.	Annual Svgs. Req. If Shortage	L21/factor	_____	$ _____

(1) See Page 2 For Factors

	ASSUMPTIONS	
23.	Years Until Retirement	_____ yrs.
24.	Years of Retirement	_____ yrs.
25.	Inflation Expectations	_____ %
26.	% Annual Incr. in Soc. Sec.	_____ %
27.	After-Tax Earnings on Invest.	
28.	Before Retirement	_____ %
29.	After Retirement	_____ %

(c) Copyright 1986 by Robert W. Shaffer

WS-I.3.3
Page 2

INSTRUCTIONS FOR COMPLETING WS-I.3.3

STEP 1. Obtain the dollar amounts to be shown on Lines 2, 3, 6, 7, 8 and 19 from previously completed work sheets. List your assumptions on Lines 23 through 29.

STEP 2. Use your assumptions to fill in the blanks under the column labeled COORDINATES on the supplemental work sheet below. Find the value of the factors by using the coordinates and the table in Exhibit 1 found at the end of Chapter 3, Section 1. Show the factor on the proper line on WS-I.3.3, Page 1.

SUPPLEMENTAL WORK SHEET

	COORDINATES	TABLE	FACTOR	SHOW ON LINE OF WS-I.3.3, PAGE 1
% Aft-Tx Earn Aft Retir. ____%	Yrs. of Ret. ____ Yrs.	A	_____	11 (If 1st Yr Deficit) 17 (If 1st Yr Surplus)
% Inflation ____%	Yrs. of Ret. ____ Yrs.	D-1	_____	13
% S.S. Incr. ____%	Yrs. of Ret. ____ Yrs.	D-1	_____	15

AFT-TX EARN AFT RET (___%) minus INFL ASSUMPTION (___%) = ____%
(DIFFERENCE)

IF DIFFERENCE IS ZERO
The Factor Is			1.0	14

IF DIFFERENCE MORE THAN ZERO
More By: ____%	Yrs. of Ret. ____ yrs.	D-2	_____	14

IF THE DIFFERENCE IS LESS THAN ZERO
Less By: ____%	Yrs. of Ret. ____ yrs.	D-3	_____	14
% Aft-Tx Earn Before Ret. ____%	Yrs. Until Retirement ____ yrs.	B	_____	20
% Aft-Tx Earn Before Ret. ____%	Yrs. Until Retirement ____ yrs.	C	_____	22

STEP 3. Complete the mathematical calculations called for in the instructions on WS-I.3.3, Page 1.

WS-I.4.1

PERSONAL EXPENSE BUDGET

Prepared for: _____

Date: _____

HOUSING		TRANSPORTATION	
Mortgage Pmt. or Rent	$ _____	Car Payments & Ins.	$ _____
Taxes and Insurance	_____	Gas, Oil & Maint	_____
Upkeep	_____	Other Trans.	_____
Utilities	_____	TOTAL TRANS.	$ _____
TOTAL HOUSING EXP.	$ _____		

FOOD		RECREATION	
Groceries & Misc.	$ _____	Vacation & Travel	$ _____
Dining Out	_____	Other Recreation	_____
TOTAL FOOD	$ _____	TOTAL RECREATION	$ _____

CLOTHING			
		LIFE INSURANCE	$ _____
New Clothes	$ _____	MED & MED INS	$ _____
Cleaning	_____	GIFTS & CHARITIES	$ _____
		OTHER EXPENSES	$ _____
TOTAL CLOTHING	$ _____		

TOTAL BUDGETED EXPENSES $ _____

INFLATION-IMPACTED EXPENSES $ _____

INFLATION-FREE EXPENSES $ _____

WS-I.4.2
Page 1

FINANCIAL PLAN
FOR RETIREMENT

Name _____   Date _____
                                Base
                                Year

Line	RETIREMENT BUDGET		
1.	INCOME		
2.	Pension		$ _____
3.	Soc. Sec.		_____
4.	Total Income	L2 + L3	_____
5.	EXPENSE		
6.	Inflation Free		_____
7.	Inc. Tx. (Pens. & Soc. Sec.)		_____
8.	Inflation-Impacted		_____
9.	Total Expense	L6 + L7 + L8	_____
10.	DEFICIT OR SURPLUS	L4 - L9	$ _____

INVESTMENT REQUIRED   Factor(1)

11.	To Cover First-Year Deficit	L10/factor	_____	$ _____
12.	To Cover Incr. Infl.-Impacted Exp.		_____	_____
13.	Impacted Expense Only	L8 x factor	_____	_____
14.	If Aft-Tx Earn is not = Infl.	L13 x factor	_____	_____
15.	Soc. Sec. Contribution	L3 x factor	_____	_____
16.	Net Required	L14 - L15	_____	_____
17.	First-Year Surplus Contribution	L10/factor	_____	(_____)
18.	TOTAL INVESTMENT REQUIRED	L16 + L11 or L16 - L17		_____

YOUR PLAN

19.	Existing Investments		$ _____
20.	Investments Required	L18	_____
21.	Excess (Shortage) of Investments	L20 - L18	_____
22.	Invest. By End of Planning Period	L21/factor _____	$ _____

(1) See Page 2
ASSUMPTIONS   For Factors
23. Years of Retirement   _____ yrs.
24. Inflation Expectations   _____ %
25. % Annual Incr. in Soc. Sec. _____ %
26. After-Tax Earnings on Invest.
27.   After Retirement   _____ %

(c) Copyright 1986 by Robert W. Shaffer

245

WS-I.4.2
Page 2

INSTRUCTIONS FOR COMPLETING WS-I.4.2

STEP 1. Obtain the dollar amounts to be shown on Lines 2, 3, 6, 7, 8 from previously completed work sheets. List your assumptions on Lines 23 through 27.

STEP 2. Use your assumptions to fill in the blanks under the column labeled COORDINATES on the supplemental work sheet below. Find the value of the factors by using the coordinates and the table in Exhibit 1 found at the end of Chapter 3, Section 1. Show the factor on the proper line on WS-I.3.3, Page 1.

SUPPLEMENTAL WORK SHEET

	COORDINATES		TABLE	FACTOR	SHOW ON LINE OF WS-I.4.2, PAGE 1
% Aft-Tx Earn Aft Retir.		Yrs. of Ret.			
____ %		____ Yrs.	A	_____	11 (If 1st Yr Deficit)
					17 (If 1st Yr Surplus)
% Inflation		Yrs. of Ret.			
____ %		____ Yrs.	D-1	_____	13
% S.S. Incr.		Yrs. of Ret.			
____ %		____ Yrs.	D-1	_____	15

AFT-TX EARN AFT RET (___%) minus INFL ASSUMPTION (___%) = ___%
                                                                                          (DIFFERENCE)

IF DIFFERENCE IS ZERO
The Factor Is   1.0   14

IF DIFFERENCE MORE THAN ZERO

More By:	Yrs. of Ret.			
____ %	____ yrs.	D-2	_____	14

IF THE DIFFERENCE IS LESS THAN ZERO

Less By:	Yrs. of Ret.			
____ %	____ yrs.	D-3	_____	14

% Aft-Tx Earn After Ret.	Yrs. of Retirement			
____ %	____ yrs.	B	_____	22

STEP 3. Complete the mathematical calculations called for in the instructions on WS-I.4.2, Page 1.

WS-I.5.1
Page 1

MY INVESTMENT ALTERNATIVES AND STRATEGIES FOR _____
                                                        (date)

MY PROFILE
    Age   _____ Yrs.
    Est. Taxable Inc. For Coming Yr. $ _____
    Before Tax Return Required to
    Protect Purchasing Power
        Ordinary Income   _____ %
        L.T. Capital Gains   _____ %
    Est. Savings to Be Inv. This Yr. $ _____

INVESTMENT GRID STRATEGY

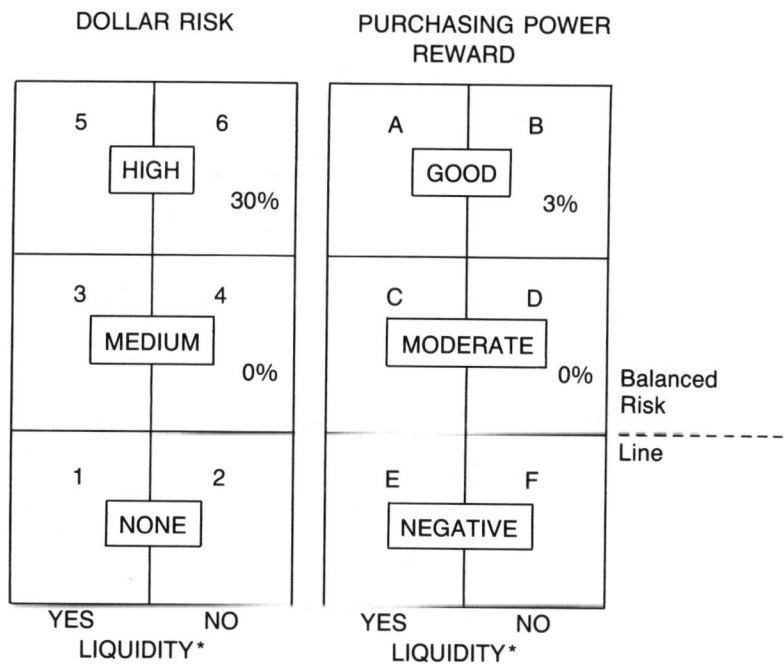

Balanced Risk Line — After-tax earnings required to protect purchasing power.

*Liquidity — The ability to redeem an asset at any time without the loss of principal and/or earnings.

WS-I.5.1
Page 2

MY EXISTING INVESTMENTS

TYPE OF INVESTMENTS	DOLLARS INVESTED	GRID CATEGORY
1.	$	
2.		
3.		
4.		
5.		
6.		
7.		
8.		
9.		
10.		

INVESTMENTS BEING CONSIDERED

TYPE OF INVESTMENT

1. _____
2. _____
3. _____
4. _____
5. _____

ACTION TO BE TAKEN TO INCREASE BY KNOWLEDGE OF INVESTING

TYPE OF ACTION

1. _____
2. _____
3. _____
4. _____
5. _____

WS-I.6.1

CONTINGENCY AND ALTERNATIVE PLANS

CONTINGENCY PLANS

Due to changes beyond my control, my plan may not materialize as I have foreseen. I will prepare contingency plans to give me insight into how these changes may affect my basic plan.

ASSUMPTIONS USED	BASIC PLAN	CONTINGENCY PLAN
Inflation	_____	_____
Longevity	_____	_____
Promotions	_____	_____
Health	_____	_____
Inheritance	_____	_____
Other _____	_____	_____
_____	_____	_____

I will prepare the following contingency plans:

1. _____
2. _____
3. _____
4. _____
5. _____

ALTERNATIVE PLANS

Due to changes beyond my control, I will prepare alternative plans to allow me the option of making other choices relative to my retirement.

FACTS USED	BASIC PLAN	CONTINGENCY PLAN
Retirement Age	_____	_____
Retirement Budget	_____	_____
Retirement Housing	_____	_____
Other _____	_____	_____
_____	_____	_____

I will prepare the following alternative plans:

1. _____
2. _____
3. _____
4. _____
5. _____

WS-I.7.1

MONITORING PROGRESS

REVIEW OF	START	COMPLETE
Net Worth	_____	_____
Facts and Assumptions	_____	_____
Basic Plan	_____	_____
Alternative & Contingency Plans	_____	_____
Investment Alternatives & Strategies	_____	_____

CRITIQUE OF PAST YEAR'S RESULTS

SUCCESSES _____

_____

_____

_____

_____

FAILURES _____

_____

_____

_____

_____

CONCLUSIONS _____

_____

_____

_____

_____

WS-II.2.1
Page 1

MY TRANSITION TO RETIREMENT

Present

My Company as a Place to Work	Yes	No
I have good supervision.	( )	( )
The working conditions are good.	( )	( )
My co-workers are friendly.	( )	( )
My pay and benefits are good.	( )	( )

My Job

	Yes	No
My job is important.	( )	( )
The company and my supervisor appreciate my contribution.	( )	( )
My work is challenging.	( )	( )
I am given assignments that are interesting.	( )	( )
I feel that I am increasing my knowledge & abilities.	( )	( )

Overall I would classify myself as

Unhappy with my job	( )	( )
Happy with my job but unmotivated	( )	( )
Happy with my job and motivated	( )	( )

After Retirement

My Anticipated Contentment with Retirement	Yes	No	Don't Know
I will be happy with the community, climate, and type of housing I have selected for retirement.	( )	( )	( )
I believe my spouse and I will have a good relationship after I retire.	( )	( )	( )
I anticipate having an active social life.	( )	( )	( )
I will have adequate financial resources.	( )	( )	( )
I like myself and am not dependent on others for my sense of self-worth.	( )	( )	( )

My Planed Retirement Activities

I plan to engage in the following hobbies:

_____ _____ _____

_____ _____ _____

	Yes	No	Don't Know
I will find these stimulating and rewarding	( )	( )	( )

WS-II.2.1
Page 2

I will satisfy my need for intellectual stimulation by:

_____

_____

_____

	Yes	No	Don't Know
These activities will satisfy my intellectual needs	( )	( )	( )

I plan to make the following contributions to society:

_____

_____

_____

	Yes	No	Don't Know
Retirees can make an important contribution to society	( )	( )	( )
I believe I will find retirement is the high point of my life	( )	( )	( )

OVERALL I THINK MY RETIREMENT WILL BE A TIME OF

	Yes	No	Don't Know
Unhappiness	( )	( )	( )
Contentment but with no zest for life	( )	( )	( )
Having zest for life	( )	( )	( )

WS-II.2.1
Page 3

TRANSITION EXPECTED

PRESENT	To	UPON RETIREMENT		TYPE OF TRANSITION
(Check the transition expected)				
Unhappiness		Unhappiness	( )	1.
Unhappiness		Contentment	( )	2.
Unhappiness		Zest for Life	( )	3.
Happy		Unhappiness	( )	4.
Happy		Contentment	( )	5.
Happy		Zest for Life	( )	6.
Motivated		Unhappiness	( )	7.
Motivated		Contentment	( )	8.
Motivated		Zest for Life	( )	9.

Thoughts as to what action I should take to better prepare myself for a retirement that would provide my life with zest.

_____
_____
_____
_____
_____
_____
_____
_____
_____
_____
_____

WS-II.3.1
Page 1

SOCIAL SKILLS INVENTORY

INTERESTS OR ACTIVITIES I HAVE THAT PROMOTE SOCIAL CONTACTS

1. _____
2. _____
3. _____
4. _____
5. _____

INTERESTS OR ACTIVITIES I WISH TO DEVELOP THAT WILL LEAD TO SOCIAL CONTACTS

1. _____
2. _____
3. _____
4. _____
5. _____

MY RATING AS A GOOD LISTENER
5 = Listens intently and asks questions to fully understand the other person's viewpoint.
1 = Does not really listen but is usually thinking about what he or she is going to say when there is a break in the conversation.

(Circle the most appropriate rating.)

MY OPINION   1   2   3   4   5

SPOUSES OPINION   1   2   3   4   5

ATTRIBUTES I HAVE THAT I CAN SHARE WITH A FRIEND
(examples — humor, empathy, hobbies, skills)

1. _____
2. _____
3. _____
4. _____
5. _____

WS-II.3.1
Page 2

ATTRIBUTES I WOULD LIKE TO HAVE IN A FRIEND

1. _____
2. _____
3. _____
4. _____
5. _____

MY PLAN TO IMPROVE MY SOCIAL SKILLS IS AS FOLLOWS:

_____
_____
_____
_____
_____
_____
_____
_____
_____
_____
_____
_____
_____
_____
_____
_____
_____
_____
_____
_____
_____
_____
_____
_____
_____

WS-II.4.1
Page 1

MY SELF-ESTEEM GAP

I. If someone asked me, "Who Are You?" I would answer:

1. _____
2. _____
3. _____
4. _____
5. _____
6. _____
7. _____
8. _____
9. _____
10. _____

II. My spouse (friend) is: (To be completed by your spouse or friend about you)

1. _____
2. _____
3. _____
4. _____
5. _____

III. The following are some of the qualities I wish I had but do not feel I possess:

1. _____
2. _____
3. _____
4. _____
5. _____

WS-II.4.1
Page 2

IV. My plan for closing my self-esteem gap is as follows:

WS-II.5.1
Page 1

MY REASON FOR BEING

I. Events in my life that brought me a sense of accomplishment

1. _____
2. _____
3. _____
4. _____
5. _____
6. _____
7. _____
8. _____
9. _____
10. _____

II. Events in my life that brought unhappiness or disappointment

1. _____
2. _____
3. _____
4. _____
5. _____
6. _____
7. _____
8. _____
9. _____
10. _____

III. Goals and/or fantasies I have had

	Goal or Fantasay	Reason for Goal
1.	_____	_____
2.	_____	_____
3.	_____	_____
4.	_____	_____
5.	_____	_____

WS-II.5.1
Page 2

IV. My Life Story (1000 words or less)

WS-II.6.1
Page 1

TACTICAL PLAN

I. My Spiritual Rating

Rating Scale: (1) = Self-centered   (10) = Concerned for mankind
(Circle the number that best describes you and explain.)

1. _____
2. _____
3. _____
4. _____
5. _____
6. _____
7. _____
8. _____
9. _____
10. _____

II. Interests

Rating Scale   (L) Low   (M) Medium   (H) High

Interest	Self	Spouse
1. _____	_____	_____
2. _____	_____	_____
3. _____	_____	_____
4. _____	_____	_____
5. _____	_____	_____
6. _____	_____	_____
7. _____	_____	_____
8. _____	_____	_____
9. _____	_____	_____
10. _____	_____	_____

WS-II.6.1
Page 2

III. Planned Retirement Activities — HOURS PER WEEK

Intellectual Stimulation

1. _____ _____
2. _____ _____
3. _____ _____
4. _____ _____
5. _____ _____
   TOTAL _____

Physical Stimulation

1. _____ _____
2. _____ _____
3. _____ _____
4. _____ _____
5. _____ _____
   TOTAL _____

Social/Spiritual Stimulation

1. _____ _____
2. _____ _____
3. _____ _____
4. _____ _____
5. _____ _____
   TOTAL _____

WS-III.5.1
Page 1

EVALUATION OF MY STATE OF WELLNESS
AND MY PLAN FOR IMPROVEMENT

I. Spiritual Health

   1. Complete the following statement with a description that reflects your ultimate concern.

      After I die, I would like for my family and friends to say that I was:

      _____

      _____

      _____

   2. Mark the answer that best reflects your approach to problems.

      My feelings as to the control I have over my life are:

      ( ) I see life as a series of challenges which give me an opportunity to grow as a person.
      ( ) I see life as a series of problems. I try to cope with them to the best of my ability.
      ( ) I see life as a series of problems which I try to avoid if at all possible.

   3. Mark the answer that best describes you self-image.

      My feelings about myself are:

      ( ) I like myself. I am human and have my faults, but I recognize them and I am making progress in becoming the person I want to be.
      ( ) The person I am and the person I want to be are two different people. I don't think people would like me if they really knew me.
      ( ) I really don't know who I am. I try to be what I think my family and friends want me to be.

WS-III.5.1
Page 2

II. Emotional Health

1. Identification of the events in my life which create stress

Event	Scale of Impact
	100
	10

2. Future events in my life (within the next two years) that may create stress

Event	Est. Scale of Impact

WS-III.5.1
Page 3

3. Stressful events that with a little planning I can avoid

Event	Est. Scale of Impact

Method of Avoidance

_____

_____

_____

_____

4. My plan for scheduling the stressful events in my life to avoid exceeding my adaptive capacity is as follows:

_____

_____

_____

5. Adaptive Capacity

   A. My perception of my adaptive capacity is:
      ( ) High
      ( ) Medium
      ( ) Low

   B. My physical vigor is:
      ( ) High
      ( ) Medium
      ( ) Low

   C. I have the following stability zones in my life:

   _____

   _____

   D. I would like to improve the stability in the following zones:

   _____

   _____

   E. My methods of relaxation are as follows:

   _____

   _____

   F. Methods of relaxation I would like to acquire:

   _____

   _____

   G. At present I am experiencing the following types of emotional pain that are probably stress related:

   _____

   _____

   _____

   _____

WS-III.5.1
Page 5

III. Physical Health

1. I have the following physical problems that are probably stress related:

   _____
   _____

2. My eating habits are: (Note if you estimate your intake of fat, salt, or sugar is excessive. (Also note whether you are maintaining your desirable weight.)

   _____
   _____

3. I should make the following changes in my diet:

   _____
   _____

4. I get the following amounts and types of exercise:

   _____
   _____

5. The above exercise program gives my heart muscle the proper exercise:
   ( ) Yes
   ( ) No

   If the answer is no, my plan to obtain the needed exercise to maintain a healthy heart is:

   _____
   _____

6. Other health habits I have which have the potential for creating health problems: (Include use of tobacco, excessive use of alcohol, coffee, etc.)

   _____
   _____
   _____
   _____
   _____

My overall state of wellness
Check the answer that best describes you.

Physical Health
    1. ( )   My last physical revealed no health problems. My muscular tone is good and I have a high energy level.

    2. ( )   I have some health problems. (Example: High blood pressure, ulcers, lower back pain, chronic fatigue, etc.)

    3. ( )   I have some disabilities: (Examples: Heart trouble, diabetes, arthritis, severe headaches, etc.)

Emotional Health
    1. ( )   I feel alive and vital. I worry very little and awake each morning eager to face the new day.

    2. ( )   I often feel tense and experience bouts of anxiety or depression. I am frequently irritable. I sometimes fantasize that it would be nice to "chuck it all" and go back to the simple life.

    3. ( )   My life is difficult. I rely upon mood-altering drugs such as alcohol, tranquilizers, etc., to cope with life. Sometimes the thought of suicide crosses my mind.

Spiritual Health
    1. ( )   I like myself. I have a genuine concern for the welfare of others. My work and my activities are worthwhile and challenging. The world will be a better place because I was here.

    2. ( )   I like myself, but if I am entirely honest with myself, I know that a great amount of my activities and efforts are self-serving.

    3. ( )   In this life one has to look out for number one, because if you don't, no one else will.

WS-III.5.1
Page 7

MY WELLNESS PROFILE

(Circle the number that most nearly corresponds to your evaluation of your health for each of the categories on page 6.)

Physical Health	Emotional Health	Spiritual Health
1	1	1
2	2	2
3	3	3

My plan to improve my overall state of wellness (List tactical, and operational plans which provide specifics as to actions to be taken, dates to start, objectives to be obtained, etc.)

_____
_____
_____
_____
_____
_____
_____
_____
_____
_____
_____
_____
_____
_____
_____
_____
_____
_____
_____

Index

−A−

Adaptive Capacity to Stress, Increasing, 206
Advisors, Criteria for Picking Financial, 94
After-Tax Earnings on Investments, 32
Age on Investment Strategy, Impact of, 76
Alternate Plans, 101
Analysis of Financial Plan for Retirement, 33
    Inflation, 34
    Savings Program, 35
Annual Financial Inventory, 107
Annual Financial Update, 108
Assets, 9
Assumptions, 19
    Career Progression, 20
    How Long Do You Want to Work?, 21
    Inflation, Rate of, 19
    Investments, Earnings on, 20
    Longevity Outlook, 21
    Social Security benefits, Increase in, 22

−B−

Being, Understanding Our, 213
Bill Takes Inventory, 152
Bill the Baker, 61
Bill's Story, 150
Body Language, 33
Browning, Robert, 1

−C−

Cardiovascular Ailments, 199
Cardiovascular Degeneration, 188
    Exercise, Lack of, 192
    Hypertension, 191
    Placque in Arteries, 190
    Smoking, 192
    Stress, 192
Coin Flip Investment Scenario, 78
Competitor Role, 146
Contingency Plans, 99

−D−

Degenerative Disease, 188
Developing Multiple Interests, 132
Dick and Jane, 49
Digestive Ailments, 199
Diversification of Investments, 77
Dollar Risk, 83

−E−

Estate Planning, 102
Esteem Needs, 122-123
Exercise Needs, 192
Explorer Role, 145

−F−

Fight or Flight Syndrome, 198
Financial Plan for Retirement, Analysis of, 33
Friends, Turning Acquaintances into, 132
Friendships, Sources for, 132

−G−

George's Investments, 85

−H−

Health, Emotional, 182
Health, Physical, 182
Health, Spiritual, 182

Herzberg, Frederick, 124
Hierarchy of Needs, 121
   Esteem, 123
   Physiological, 122
   Safety and Security, 122
   Self-Actualization, 124
   Social or Affiliation, 123
Hobbies and Crafts, 160
Holmes and Rahe, Doctors, 200
Housing, Retirement, 12
Human Machine, The, 218
Hygiene Factors Needed for Motivation, 124
Hypertension, 191

– I –

Immune System Failure, 199
Improving Communication Skills, 132
Income Tax on Pension and Social Security, 31
Inflation, Impact on a Retirement Budget, 34
Inflation Rate, Assumption, 76
Inflation Impacted Expenses, 31
Inflation-Free Expenses, 31
Intellect, Programing of Our, 214
Intellect, Reprogramming Our, 215
Intellectual Games, 161
Intellectual Stimulation, 159
   Advisory and/or Teaching, 160
   Hobbies and Crafts, 160
   Intellectual Games, 161
   Investments, 162
   Political Activity, 161
   Second or Continued Career, 162
   Systematic Pursuit of Knowledge, 159
   Traveling, 161
Investment Alternatives, 67
   Loans, 65, 68
   An Interest in a Business, 65, 71
      Common Stock, 71
      Limited Partnership, 72
      Preferred Stock, 71
   Tangible Assets, 73

Investment Advisory Services, 90
   Investment Counselors, 93
   Market Letters and Financial Publications, 92
   Mutual Funds, 90
   Stock and Bond Brokers, 92
   Tax Attorneys — Accountants — Bankers, 93
   Trusts, 93
Investment Deficit, Dealing With an, 102
Investment Strategy, 73, 78
Investment Terminology, 65
Investments, Prudent, 162
Investments Required, 33
Investor, Attributes of Skilled, 73
   Decisiveness, 75
   Discipline To Save, 75
   Imagination, 74
   Knowledge, 74

– K –

Keeping the Proper Perspective, 109

– L –

Leverage, 66, 77
Liabilities, 9
Liquidity, 83
Listening Skills, 133
Living With the Assumptions, 36
Longevity, Estimate, 21

– M –

Marginal Tax Rate, 32, 66, 76
Maslow, Abraham, 121
Maturity, Emotional, 197
Mental Problems, 199
Mission for Life, 11
Motivation Factors, 124

Index 271

—N—

Needs, Intellectual and Social, 12
Net Worth Statement, 9

—P—

Pension Income, Estimate, 26
Pete's New Value System, 142
Pete's Story, 140
Physical Needs, 163
Physiological Needs, 122
Placque, 190
Planning for Change, 118
Planning, Operational, 175
Planning, Strategic, 173
Planning, Tactical, 174
Political Activity, 161
Provider Role, 146
Purchasing Power Reward, 84

—Q—

Quality Life, 182, 193

—R—

Reaper Role, 148
Recreation, 164
Retirement as a Source of Stress, 202
Retirement Living Costs, 28
    Clothing, 29
    Contributions to Charity, 30
    Food, 29
    Gifts, 30
    Housing, 29
    Life Insurance, 30
    Medical Expenses, 30
    Miscellaneous and Contingency, 30
    Transportation, 29
    Recreation, 29
Retirement Party, 116
Revisiting Bill, 164
Risk-Reward Grid, 82
Rites of Passage, 115

—S—

Safety or Security Needs, 122
Savings Required for Retirement, 31
Second or Continued Career, 162
Self-Actualization Needs, 122, 124
Self-esteem Gap, 139
Semantics, 133
Skeletal-Muscular Disorders, 199
Skill Inventory, 11
Smoking, Danger of, 192
Social or Affiliation Needs, 122-123
Social Readjustment Rating Scale, 200
Social Security Benefits, 26
Social Skills, 131
Spiritual Health, 213
Spiritual Stimulation, 162
Stress, 192
Stress Management Program, 204
Stressful Events, Predicting
    Future, 205

—T—

Tangible Assets, Purchasing, 65
Tax Code Provisions, 77
The Savings Program, 35
Traveling, 161

—U—

Ultimate Concern, Formulating
    Your, 217

—W—

Wellness, 181
Wellness, Plan for, 221
Wellness, Working Toward, 217

—Z—

Zest for Life, 126

BUSINESS — PROFESSIONAL BOOKS

Occupying the Summit $15.95
The Guide to Successful Retirement Plannning 1-55622-102-9
Robert W. Shaffer

With retirement now encompassing as much as 25 percent of our lifespan, this book offers sound advice for making that time the best phase of life. Practical guidance and hands-on worksheets help evaluate current status, determine goals, and develop a positive retirement strategy. Regardless of income and age level, this book provides the essential principles and foresight necessary to successfully anticipate and prepare for a financially independent, healthy, and fulfilling retirement.

How to Win Pageants $24.95
Ginie Polo Sayles 1-55622-112-6

Pageants are the number one television draw in the world today. With over 5 million participants each year, pageants now attract children, teenagers, married women, and men. *How to Win Pageants* contains inside information for a competitive edge in this exploding industry. Detailed interviews provide invaluable insights from Miss America, Miss Universe, Mr. Male America, Miss National Teenager, children's international Diamond Miss, and many others. Inside information from numerous winners and "powers behind the throne" identify what the judges look for, who the top trainers are, and where to find them. This book provides keys to people-awareness skills, positive personality projection, and physical fitness habits that can be stepping stones to success as they were for pageant winners Sophia Loren and Diane Sawyer.

Desktop Publisher's Dictionary $19.95
Larry S. Bonura 1-55622-106-1

Discover the language of desktop publishing with this comprehensive, one-stop reference to the terms used in this exploding industry. More than 4000 terms, words, and abbreviations, from typography to binding and finishing, are clearly defined and frequently clarified by illustrations. Related terms and concepts are identified for easy cross-reference. Perfect for office, home, or school, this is an indispensable tool for today's contemporary professional.

MegaTraits $17.95
Dr. Doris Lee McCoy 1-55622-056-1

Dr. McCoy traveled extensively to interview over 1,000 "successful" people. Interviews with such people as Charlton Heston, Malcolm Forbes, and Ronald Reagan led Dr. McCoy to discover 12 traits of success. She sought consistencies and success patterns from which you can benefit. Are there specific points to help all of us become more successful? The answer is a resounding YES! There are traits consistently found in the lives of successful people. Read *MegaTraits* to discover how you too can develop and utilize these unique attributes.

Business Emotions $14.95
Richard Contino 1-55622-058-8

Revolutionize your thinking, conditioning, and approach. Learn why emotions are a controlling factor in every success and failure situation. This practical book will guide you through the maze of hidden psychological issues in a simple and straightforward manner. Achieve predictable, positive, and immediate results.

Innovation, Inc. $14.95
Stephen Grossman, Bruce Rodgers, 1-55622-054-5
Beverly Moore

Unlock your hidden potential to reach a new plane of creative thinking. Seek out new avenues of problem-solving by elevating your ability to conceive ideas. Techniques and exercises in this book expand your creativity. The authors take you on a journey designed to spark confidence by reorganizing your thinking processes and patterns. Learn to use innovative thinking to inspire fresh ideas and formulate imaginative concepts.

Investor Beware $14.95
Henry Rothenberg 1-55622-055-3

Create your own luck with this book detailing the essentials for safe investments. Avoid shady, risky, and unsuccessful investments. Learn how to anticipate and interpret various investment climates and analyze a business from financial statements. The average investor will find what he needs to know about economics, financing, taxes, operating entities, and types of investments. Discover the ramifications of diversified investments such as real estate, franchises, oil and gas, gold, tax shelters, and syndications.

Steps to Strategic Management $13.95
Rick Molz 1-55622-050-2

This book is the story of one individual. . .YOU. Put yourself in the shoes of Joe Clancy, the imaginary entrepreneur in this book. By following the clear, ongoing example of Joe, you will discover how strategic management works. A series of nine steps will help you develop a systematic approach to strategic management. With honesty and hard work, you can use this book to help shape your future.

Call Wordware Publishing, Inc. for names of the bookstores in your area.
(214) 423-0090